P9-BJH-396

The NAA Standards for Quality School-Age Care

Boston, Massachusetts
1998

Copyright ©1998 by the National AfterSchool Association

All rights reserved.
Printed in the United States of America.

Edited by Janette Roman.

Design and production by David Gerratt, DG Communications, Acton, Massachusetts.
Photography by Mark Ostow, Somerville, Massachusetts.
Artwork by Carol Calabro, Acton, Massachusetts.
Printing by Puritan Press, Hollis, New Hampshire.

10   9   8   7   6   5   4   3   2

National AfterSchool Association
1137 Washington Street
Boston, Massachusetts 02124

ACKNOWLEDGMENTS

The NAA Standards for Quality School-Age Care were developed by the National AfterSchool Association, formerly the National School-Age Care Alliance, for the implementation of the National Program Improvement and Accreditation System. These Standards were made possible through collaboration with the National Institute on Out-of-School Time (formerly the SACC Project) at the Center for Research on Women at Wellesley College.

Generous support for the development of these Standards was provided by the American Business Collaboration for Quality Dependent Care, the AT&T Family Care Development Fund, the DeWitt Wallace-Reader's Digest Fund, the U.S. Air Force, and the U.S. Army. The Standards are based on the ASQ (Assessing School-Age Child Care Quality) Program Observation Instrument and Questions for the Director by Susan O'Connor, Thelma Harms, Debby Cryer, and Kathryn A. Wheeler. The Next Steps section of the Standards was developed in consultation with: Susan O'Connor, formerly from the National Institute on Out-of-School Time; Jean Berkwitt, an early childhood education consultant in Hartford, and Deb Flis of the Accreditation Facilitation Project of Hartford.

SPECIAL ACKNOWLEDGMENT IS GIVEN TO:

Linda Sisson, formerly the Executive Director of NAA, for her significant contribution in developing the NAA Standards for Quality School-Age Care, as well as the National Program Improvement and Accreditation System.

The former NAA Board of Advisors, and especially former Board President Ellen Clippinger, for their commitment and leadership throughout this endeavor.

Work-Family Directions (WFD) for providing a link to the American Business Collaboration for Quality Dependent Care; and especially NAA's liaison at WFD, Sharon Myrick, whose constant support guided and informed NAA's strategic development of the Program Improvement and Accreditation System from the pilot phase through national implementation.

The staff at the National Institute on Out-of-School Time, for its role in helping develop the Program Improvement and Accreditation System. NAA is especially thankful to former Executive Director Michelle Seligson, for her vision to develop standards and a system for program improvement; Co-Director Ellen Gannett and former Research Associate Susan O'Connor, for their contributions to the national pilot of the system; and former Project Associate Katie Wheeler, for her work on endorser reliability.

Members of the NAA Accreditation Advisory Board, who shared their wisdom and expertise in the revision of these Standards. Their thorough review has helped this work reach a broader range of afterschool programs and the families they serve. *NAA Accreditation Advisory Board Members:* Ethel Barnes, Sue Bohlen, Virginia Brown, Elaine Taylor, Deb Ukura, and Debbie Wooldridge.

NAA wishes to thank the afterschool programs who participated in the national pilot of these Standards. Their experiences and suggestions helped shape the National Program Improvement and Accreditation System.

Special thanks to the staff, children, and youth whose photographs bring the book to life. Photos were taken at the following afterschool programs: Patrick O'Hearn Elementary in Dorchester, MA; and Plowshares SACC Program in Newton, MA.

The NAA Standards were reviewed for publication by Linda Rath, Literacy Consultant. Her work helped make this text more readable and user-friendly.

This book was designed and produced by David Gerratt/DG Communications. Photographs were taken by Mark Ostow. Artwork was created by Carol Calabro.

CONTENTS

Introduction

Q & A on the Standards and the National System
of Program Improvement and Accreditation   1

How the Standards are Organized and Formatted   5

The Standards

Human Relationships   9

Indoor Environment   21

Outdoor Environment   25

Activities   27

Safety, Health, & Nutrition   33

Administration   41

Next Steps   67

Appendices

Staff Qualifications   75

Standards at a Glance   79

Glossary   89

INTRODUCTION

Today's complex world presents many challenges for children—and the adults who care for them. As school-age care professionals—and as caring adults—we seek to offer an environment in which children can grow to the best of their abilities, one which taps their creativity and strengths and allows them to excel.

The NAA Standards provide a baseline of quality, and the reassurance that programs are committed to providing each child with a unique growing and learning experience.

Q & A on the Standards and the National System of Program Improvement and Accreditation

Who wrote these Standards?

Several years of research and field testing led to the development of the *NAA Standards for Quality School-Age Care*. The pilot Standards were initially drafted by an NAA Standards Committee in 1995, and were based on the Program Observation and Questions for the Director in ASQ (Advancing School-Age Child Care Quality). This self-study guide for programs was written by Susan O'Connor, formerly from the National Institute on Out-of-School Time. NAA conducted a national field test of the pilot Standards in 1996. The Standards were revised in 1997. This most recent version includes suggestions and ideas from the pilot sites, as well as extensive review from the NAA Accreditation Advisory Board, NAA staff and school-age professionals across the country.

Why were the Standards written?

The Standards are designed to describe the best practices in out-of-school programs for children and youth between the ages of five and 14. They are intended for use in group settings where the children participate on a regular basis and where the goal of the program is to support and enhance the overall development of the child. They will be used to assess programs applying for NAA accreditation.

How will the Standards be used?

These Standards are the basis of the self-study process and of accreditation. Programs will rate themselves using these tools to make an improvement plan. Endorsers will rate the programs on these Standards when they apply for accreditation.

How can I use the Standards to assess my program?

Your first step is to read and become familiar with the NAA Standards and the examples that follow them. Reflecting on the Guiding Questions, and discussing them with the staff, families, and children in your program will help you determine:

- What are we currently doing to meet this Standard?

- What do we wish we were doing to better meet this Standard?

- Why is this Standard important?

Once you have become familiar with the Standards and understand how they apply to your program, you are ready to explore the Next Steps section of this book. This section contains a tool to help you determine the course of action that is best suited to your program. The possibilities include:

- Focusing on targeted improvements

- Beginning the full self-study process using the ASQ materials

- Deciding whether to apply for NAA Accreditation

Because each program is unique, there is no time limit for when you must complete these steps. Our goal is to provide programs with the necessary tools to make positive decisions that will improve the quality of care they provide. This is not a one-time event; it's a commitment to continuous improvement.

Why do we need an accreditation system for school-age care?

While some afterschool programs have used the National Association for the Education of Young Children (NAEYC) accreditation system, there are some unique characteristics of school-age care which no other system currently addresses:

- the wide range of ages served from five-year-olds to 14-year-olds;

- the "shared" nature of many aspects of school-age care, including sharing facilities, sharing staff with other jobs and schools, sharing children with schools and other activities, and sharing the calendar with the schools;

- and the unique combination of skills required to do the work well, including community outreach, child guidance, recreation planning, and group facilitation.

We also need a system which will help raise awareness about the importance of out-of-school time for our children and youth, and the difference that quality experiences during that time can make.

Why is this called "*Improvement* and Accreditation"?

This system is based on a method of self-study and program improvement. The National AfterSchool Association (NAA) wants to be sure that all programs can benefit from the system. Our goal is to make the Standards relevant and available to programs, even if they choose not to pursue accreditation. We also recognize that even the most outstanding programs continually work toward improvement even after accreditation.

Who developed the system?

The system was developed through a collaboration between NAA and the National Institute on Out-of-School Time (formerly the SACC Project). NAA is a representative professional membership organization, and the National Institute is an action-oriented research group. In 1997, NAA began managing the national implementation of the system. The National Institute continues to share its expertise with NAA in an advisory capacity. The Institute is also available to provide training and technical assistance to participating programs.

How was the system tested?

Seventy-five programs in 13 states representing diverse settings, sizes, agencies, and populations served as the pilot sites. All of the programs received a training in the use of the ASQ self-study materials and the process of accreditation. Sixty of the programs also participated in support groups and received some technical assistance during the 18 months of the pilot. NAA conducted a second field test of the Program Improvement and Accreditation System in North Carolina. With help from local organizations and professionals, we hope to further refine the process and procedures for NAA Accreditation. All field testing was made possible through generous funding from:

- the American Business Collaboration for Quality Dependent Care;

- the AT&T Family Care Development Fund;

- the DeWitt Wallace–Reader's Digest Fund;

- the U.S. Air Force; and

- the U.S. Army.

What did NAA learn from the pilot?

The national pilot helped NAA identify the supports programs need to be successful throughout self study and accreditation. These supports fall into three categories:

Program Supports
We learned that many programs need additional administrative support to undertake self-study and accreditation. Please refer to the Next Steps section of this book. It contains more detailed information to guide programs through continuous quality improvement.

Community Supports
We learned that established community systems are necessary to support program quality. This includes strong state licensing regulations; an established provider support network; and regular training opportunities for providers.

National Supports
We were able to identify the necessary elements for implementing a national program improvement and accreditation system. These include targeted training; a diverse pool of qualified endorsers; and the capacity to schedule and manage site visits for programs who apply for accreditation.

How can I get more information?
You can contact:

The National AfterSchool Association
1137 Washington Street
Boston, MA 02124
Tel: (617) 298-5012
Fax: (617) 298-5022
E-mail: staff@naaweb.org
Web: www.naaweb.org

HOW THE STANDARDS ARE ORGANIZED AND FORMATTED

Format of the Standards

- On each page there is one *key*.
- Next to each key there are *guiding questions*.
- Under each key there are specific *standards*.
- With most standards there are *examples*.

Here's how it looks:

KEY

2. Staff respond appropriately to the individual needs of children and youth.

STANDARD

Staff know that each child has special interests and talents.

EXAMPLES

Staff are able to spend time with individual children. Staff bring in materials related to children's interests: pets, music, sports, computers, chess, etc. Specialists are used for certain activities. Staff are eager to hear about events in children's lives outside the program.

GUIDING QUESTIONS:

Are we aware of the many interests, abilities, and talents of our children?

How do we respond to their different cultures and languages?

The *examples* are illustrations of the kinds of things to look for when using the Standards to evaluate your program. You would not necessarily find all of those specific examples at your program. You may be meeting the standard in another way.

NOTE:
Words that appear in **purple** are defined in the Glossary.

Organization of the Standards

There are thirty-six **keys of quality** in the NAA Standards. Twenty of the keys are observable and are organized under five categories.

Human Relationships

1. Staff relate to all children and youth in positive ways.

2. Staff respond appropriately to the individual needs of children and youth.

3. Staff encourage children and youth to make choices and to become more responsible.

4. Staff interact with children and youth to help them learn.

5. Staff use positive techniques to guide the behavior of children and youth.

6. Children and youth generally interact with one another in positive ways.

7. Staff and families interact with each other in positive ways.

8. Staff work well together to meet the needs of children and youth.

Indoor Environment

9. The program's indoor space meets the needs of children and youth.

10. The indoor space allows children and youth to take initiative and explore their interests.

Outdoor Environment

11. The outdoor play area meets the needs of children and youth, and the equipment allows them to be independent and creative.

Activities

12. The daily schedule is flexible, and it offers enough security, independence, and stimulation to meet the needs of all children and youth.

13. Children and youth can choose from a wide variety of activities.

14. Activities reflect the mission of the program and promote the development of all the children and youth in the program.

15. There are sufficient materials to support program activities.

Safety, Health, & Nutrition

16. The safety and security of children and youth are protected.

17. The program provides an environment that protects and enhances the health of children and youth.

18. The program staff try to protect and enhance the health of children and youth.

19. Children and youth are carefully supervised to maintain safety.

20. The program serves foods and drinks that meet the needs of children and youth.

Sixteen additional keys describe the program organization, procedures, and policies. Together they create a sixth category of Administration.

Administration

21. Staff/child ratios and group sizes permit the staff to meet the needs of children and youth.

22. Children and youth are supervised at all times.

23. Staff support families' involvement in the program.

24. Staff, families, and schools share important information to support the well-being of children and youth.

25. The program builds links to the community.

26. The program's indoor space meets the needs of staff.

27. The outdoor space is large enough to meet the needs of children, youth, and staff.

28. Staff, children, and youth work together to plan and implement suitable activities, which are consistent with the program's philosophy.

29. Program policies and procedures are in place to protect the safety of the children and youth.

30. Program policies exist to protect and enhance the health of all children and youth.

31. All staff are professionally qualified to work with children and youth.

32. Staff (paid, volunteer, and substitute) are given an orientation to the job before working with children and youth.

33. The training needs of the staff are assessed, and training is relevant to the responsibilities of each job. Assistant Group Leaders receive at least 15 hours of training annually. Group Leaders receive at least 18 hours of training annually. Senior Group Leaders receive at least 21 hours of training annually. Site Directors receive at least 24 hours of training annually. Program Administrators receive at least 30 hours of training annually.

34. Staff receive appropriate support to make their work experience positive.

35. The administration provides sound management of the program.

36. Program policies and procedures are responsive to the needs of children, youth, and families in the community.

HUMAN
RELATIONSHIPS

HUMAN RELATIONSHIPS

1. Staff relate to all children and youth in positive ways.

GUIDING
QUESTIONS:

How do we
greet children?

Are they happy
to be with us?

Do we feel
we have
enough time
to talk with
individual and
small groups
of children
every day?

What else can
we do to help
children in our
program feel
welcome?

Staff treat children with respect and listen to what they say.
Staff do not belittle children. They take children's comments seriously. Staff do not intrude or interrupt children. Staff use supportive language. They make statements like "Keep trying; you can do it!"

Staff make children feel welcome and comfortable.
Staff project a tone of welcome in their voices and gestures. Staff acknowledge children when they arrive and depart. They respond appropriately when children show affection. Staff stay calm in all situations. They handle conflicts in a way that reduces fear or disruption.

Staff respond to children with acceptance and appreciation.
Staff are kind and fair to all children. They include all interested children in activities and events. Games and sports are open to all, regardless of their athletic skill. Staff do not separate children by gender. They do not discriminate on the basis of race, religion, gender, ethnicity, family structure, appearance, disability, etc.

Staff are engaged with children.
Staff talk and play with the children. They show interest in what the children say and do. Staff participate in many activities with children. Staff sit with children at snack time. Staff show that they enjoy children. Staff seem cheerful rather than bored, tired, or distant. Staff spend little time on tasks that do not involve the children.

NOTE:
Words that appear in **purple** are defined in the Glossary.

2. Staff respond appropriately to the individual needs of children and youth.

Staff know that each child has special interests and talents.
Staff are able to spend time with individual children. Staff bring in materials related to children's interests: pets, music, sports, computers, chess, etc. Specialists are used for certain activities. Staff are eager to hear about events in children's lives outside the program.

Staff recognize the range of children's abilities.
Staff vary their responses to match children's ages and abilities. Staff help children become focused and engaged. Staff help children pursue their interests and improve their skills. Staff offer enrichment activities. Staff help children with their homework. Staff substitute equipment as needed, such as using a large beach ball instead of a volleyball for outdoor games.

Staff can relate to a child's culture and home language.
Staff provide resources that show different cultural perspectives. They help children use books, music, and tapes in different languages. Visual displays show a variety of cultures. Signs include the home languages of the children in the program. Children have an opportunity to speak their home language with peers and staff. Guests from various cultural traditions are invited to speak at the program and share their experiences. They also serve as coaches, mentors, and friends.

Key 2
continued next page

GUIDING QUESTIONS:

Are we aware of the many interests, abilities, and talents of our children?

How do we respond to their different cultures and languages?

In what other ways can we help each child grow and learn?

HUMAN RELATIONSHIPS

Key 2
*continued from
previous page*

2. Staff respond appropriately to the individual needs of children and youth.

Staff respond to the range of children's feelings and temperaments.

Staff try to understand the different ways children express their feelings (e.g., different cultural styles to show respect for authority, express hurt or anger or warmth). Staff try to assess children's feelings before attempting to solve a problem. Staff find suitable ways to include all children. Staff accept a child's desire to be alone. Staff remain calm and patient with an angry child. Staff comfort a child who appears hurt, upset, or disappointed.

3. Staff encourage children and youth to make choices and to become more responsible.

Staff offer assistance in a way that supports a child's initiative.
Staff help children find ways to pursue their own interests. Staff say "yes" to children's reasonable requests and ideas for activities. Staff help children plan projects and gather resources.

Staff assist children without taking control, and they encourage children to take leadership roles.
Staff give clear directions so that children can proceed independently. When asked, staff step in to help children. Staff encourage children to proceed on their own.

Staff give children many chances to choose what they will do, how they will do it, and with whom.
Children have frequent opportunities to choose their companions. Children help prepare and/or serve their own food. Children set up activities and/or clean up afterwards. Older children may choose to set up their own clubhouse. When field trips are planned, some children may choose to stay at the program.

Staff help children make informed and responsible choices.
Staff remind children to think about how their actions may affect others in the program. Staff ask questions that guide children to make good decisions. Staff help children understand the impact of their decisions on others.

GUIDING QUESTIONS:

What kinds of choices can children in our program make?

How often do we let them choose what they are going to do, and with whom?

Are we helping them to take initiative and assume leadership roles? Do we include children when we plan activities?

NOTE: Words that appear in **purple** are defined in the Glossary.

HUMAN RELATIONSHIPS

4. Staff interact with children and youth to help them learn.

GUIDING
QUESTIONS:

What kinds of
questions do
we ask chil-
dren to encour-
age creative
thinking? How
do we respond
to children's
curiosity?

What ap-
proaches do
we use to
answer their
questions?

How do we
help children
reflect on what
they are
learning?

Staff ask questions that encourage children to think for themselves.

Staff pursue children's ideas. Staff start discussions by asking open-ended questions (e.g., "what if?" or "how can we…?"). Staff encourage children to use journal writing, art projects and group discussions as a way to express their ideas. Staff take time to think about children's questions.

Staff share skills and resources to help children gain information and solve problems.

Staff show children how and where to find answers to questions. Staff show children how complex skills can be broken into smaller steps. Staff encourage children to practice basic life skills. When children face problems they cannot solve themselves, staff offer suggestions.

Staff vary the approaches they use to help children learn.

Staff teach children a new task or game by showing the steps as well as telling about them. Staff write down instructions for activities so that children can remember what to do. Staff pay attention to culture and gender variations in learning styles. They recognize non-verbal as well as verbal responses. They encourage children to try new activities. They help children move beyond gender stereotypes in their choices. Staff use pictures and visual aids to reach out to non-readers and speakers of other languages. Staff modify activities as needed so that all children, including those with disabilities, can participate.

Staff help children use language skills through frequent conversations.

Staff speak to children on a level children seem to understand. They listen patiently as all children try to express themselves. Staff take extra time with children who speak another language at home or have difficulty listening or speaking. Staff try to find effective ways to communicate with all children. Staff sometimes use non-verbal signals to help children understand.

GUIDING QUESTIONS:

Are we able to work with individual children who need our help and support throughout the day?

NOTE: Words that appear in **purple** are defined in the Glossary.

HUMAN RELATIONSHIPS

5. Staff use positive techniques to guide the behavior of children and youth.

GUIDING
QUESTIONS:

How do we
model caring,
cooperation,
and respect?

Can we iden-
tify a pattern
for the types
of conflict that
occur most
often?

Are there times
when conflicts
are most likely
to occur? Are
there simple
changes we
can make to
prevent these
conflicts from
occurring?

What methods
do we use to
help children
resolve their
conflicts?

Staff give attention to children when they cooperate, share, care for materials, or join in activities.
Staff often show appreciation and encouragement. They avoid using insincere praise and threats to control children's behavior. Staff teach children how to communicate and cooperate. Staff celebrate children's efforts and progress.

Staff set appropriate limits for children.
Staff set limits to prevent children from hurting each other physically or verbally. If children tease, scapegoat, threaten, or exclude others, staff step in. Staff avoid setting unrealistic limits, such as expecting children to be quiet most of the day. Staff take steps to ensure that each child understands the limits that are set.

Staff use no harsh discipline methods.
Staff do not shame, yell, hit, or withhold food. The whole group is not scolded or punished when one child breaks a rule. Staff avoid correcting children publicly. Staff do not force children to explain their behavior or apologize.

Staff encourage children to resolve their own conflicts. Staff step in only if needed to discuss the issues and work out a solution.
Staff listen and observe carefully. Staff use negotiation, reasoning, and redirection to help children find alternatives. Staff do not impose their solutions on children. Staff rarely lecture children. Staff help children express their feelings. Staff help children understand how their behavior affects others. Staff teach children specific skills to work through conflicts (e.g., circle time, peace table, or conflict-resolution skills).

6. Children and youth generally interact with one another in positive ways.

Children appear relaxed and involved with each other.
Group sounds are pleasant most of the time.

Children show respect for each other.
Teasing, belittling, or picking on particular children is uncommon. Children show sympathy for each other and help each other.

Children usually cooperate and work well together.
Children willingly share materials and space. They suggest activities, negotiate roles, and jointly work out the rules. Children include others with developmental, physical, or language differences in their play. Children often help each other. There is a strong sense of community.

When problems occur, children often try to discuss their differences and work out a solution.
Children listen to each other's point of view and try to compromise (e.g., if two children want to use the same equipment, they may decide to take turns as a solution). Children know how to solve problems. Their solutions are usually reasonable and fair. They do not try to solve disagreements by bullying or acting aggressively.

GUIDING QUESTIONS:

Do children seem to enjoy spending time together?

Do they talk about friends at the program?

Do they tend to include others from different backgrounds, or with different abilities in their play?

NOTE:
Words that appear in **purple** are defined in the Glossary.

HUMAN RELATIONSHIPS

7. Staff and families interact with each other in positive ways.

GUIDING
QUESTIONS:

How do we help our families feel welcome and comfortable?

Do we know enough about our families?

Do families from all backgrounds seem to be involved and connected?

Staff make families feel welcome and comfortable.
> Staff and family members greet one another by name. Staff use friendly voices, expressions, and gestures. They are relaxed and not abrupt with each other.

Staff and families treat each other with respect.
> Staff and family members show interest in each other's lives. Respect is shown to all without bias. Staff communicate with families in a variety of ways. Staff recognize that some cultures like direct communication, while others prefer indirect. Staff do not talk about confidential matters in front of the children or other adults.

Staff share the languages and cultures of the families they serve, and the communities they live in.
> The program's diverse staff reflect the cultures and languages of the children in the program. Whenever possible, staff speak with families in their home language. Staff ask translators to help communicate with families during individual and large-group meetings. Staff avoid using children as translators if possible. Staff provide information written in the family's home language. Displays and signs reflect the diversity in the community.

Staff and families work together to make arrivals and departures between home and childcare go smoothly.
> Family members can easily find their children and their children's possessions. Conversations with family members do not take attention away from children or their activities.

NOTE:
Words that appear in **purple** are defined in the Glossary.

8. Staff work well together to meet the needs of children and youth.

Staff communicate with each other while the program is in session to ensure that the program flows smoothly.

Staff check with each other to make sure all areas are supervised. Conversations about personal matters are brief and do not interfere with transitions and activities.

Staff are cooperative with each other.

Staff are flexible about their roles. They pitch in to help each other with the children as needed. Work appears to be shared fairly. When problems occur, staff discuss their differences and work toward fair solutions. Long or complicated discussions are saved for times when children are not present.

Staff are respectful of each other.

Respect is shown to all. Staff communicate their needs in a way that promotes cooperation. Staff are aware of how their tone and demeanor convey respect. They manage tense situations in a way that shows respect for other staff members.

Staff provide role models of positive adult relationships.

Staff check in with each other and stay in touch throughout the day. Staff model positive adult interaction through cooperation, caring, and effective communication. Staff notice and respond supportively to non-verbal cues and gestures.

GUIDING QUESTIONS:

How do we support each other in meeting the needs of children?

Do we set examples of positive adult relationships?

Do we set time aside to review our plans? Do we find chances to share our ideas?

INDOOR ENVIRONMENT

INDOOR ENVIRONMENT

9. The program's indoor space meets the needs of children and youth.

GUIDING
QUESTIONS:

Do we use all
of the space
available to us
throughout the
program day?

How do chil-
dren make use
of the indoor
space?

Are there
certain areas
they avoid?

Do other
areas seem
overcrowded?

How do we
maximize the
use of shared
space?

There is enough room for all program activities.
> Children can work and play without crowding. There is
> enough space so that indoor activities do not interfere with
> each other. There is indoor space for active play during
> bad weather.

The space is arranged well for a range of activities: physical
games and sports, creative arts, dramatic play, quiet games,
enrichment offerings, eating, and socializing.
> Messy play takes place near the sink or by a floor that is
> easy to wash. Materials are sorted and well organized.
> Running water is conveniently located.

The space is arranged so that various activities can go
on at the same time without much disruption.
> Active play does not disrupt quiet play (e.g., loud music
> does not distract children doing homework). Pathways
> allow children to move from one place to another without
> disturbing ongoing activities. Sharing the space with other
> groups (e.g. schools or churches) does not restrict the
> children's activities or noise level.

There is adequate and convenient storage space for
equipment, materials, and personal possessions of children
and staff.
> There is a place for children and staff to store personal
> belongings. Materials used frequently and works-in-
> progress are accessible to children. There are other places
> to store bulk materials and things not currently in use.

NOTE:
Words that
appear in **purple**
are defined in
the Glossary.

10. The indoor space allows children and youth to take initiative and explore their interests.

Children can get materials out and put them away by themselves with ease.

Materials that see frequent use are kept on low and open shelves. Materials and supplies are equally accessible to all children. If supply cabinets are locked, they can be opened for use while children are at the program.

Children can arrange materials and equipment to suit their activities.

Children can choose tables and desks that are at the right height for their size and activity. Children can sit comfortably without being cramped (e.g., with feet on the floor and arms on the table). Children can move furniture easily to make more room or to define an area.

The indoor space reflects the work and interests of the children.

Displays feature children's artwork and other pictures of interest to them. Children are free to personalize the space and redefine some areas for their purposes (e.g., to build "forts" or clubhouses.) The decor portrays people from different ethnic and racial backgrounds engaged in a variety of roles.

Some areas have soft, comfortable furniture on which children can relax.

Children can use couches, cushions, beanbag chairs, or rugs. There are some spaces that suit children who want to rest or be alone.

GUIDING QUESTIONS:

Are the program's resources accessible to children?

Do children have enough of a chance to explore their own interests?

How are their interests and work visible throughout the indoor space?

OUTDOOR ENVIRONMENT

OUTDOOR ENVIRONMENT

11. The outdoor play area meets the needs of children and youth, and the equipment allows them to be independent and creative.

GUIDING
QUESTIONS:

**When we set
the outdoor
schedule, do
we follow the
interests of
the staff or
the children?**

**Have we
explored ways
to offer more
opportunities
for outdoor
play?**

**Do we have
convenient
storage for
outdoor
equipment?**

Each child has a chance to play outdoors for at least 30 minutes out of every three-hour block of time at the program.
> When weather permits, children can go outdoors often. In some situations, all children may go outdoors to play. In others, outdoor play can be offered as an open-ended choice. An indoor space is available for large-motor activities when the weather is bad (e.g., extreme cold, heat, or smog alert).

Children can use a variety of outdoor equipment and games for both active and quiet play.
> Storage areas are kept open so that children may select play equipment. Outdoor games and sports equipment are stored close to the play space.

Permanent playground equipment is suitable for the sizes and abilities of all children.
> Equipment offers various levels of challenge. Older children have access to more challenging equipment. Younger children can reach most of the climbing structures. Equipment is accessible for use by children with disabilities. For example: There are enough ramps and paved areas for children in wheelchairs to be able to use the playground.

The outdoor space is suitable for a wide variety of activities.
> There is an open area where children can run, jump, and play. There is a protected area for quiet play and socializing. There is a large ball field area. There is a hard surface for basketball, rollerskating, and bike riding.

NOTE:
Words that
appear in **purple**
are defined in
the Glossary.

ACTIVITIES

ACTIVITIES

12. The daily schedule is flexible, and it offers enough security, independence, and stimulation to meet the needs of all children and youth.

GUIDING
QUESTIONS:

Does our system allow children to move at their own pace from one activity to another?

When is it necessary for all the children to participate in the same activity?

Is snack time handled in a relaxed and flexible way?

The routine provides stability without being rigid.

Children seem to know the daily routine and to follow it without many reminders. Large-group outdoor time is extended or shortened, depending on the weather and the interest of the children. Time is set aside to discuss rules. Staff and children work together to define rules that make sense to all.

Children meet their physical needs in a relaxed way.

Children can get drinks and go to the bathroom without waiting for the group. Children can have a snack as an activity choice instead of eating together as a large group.

Individual children move smoothly from one activity to another, usually at their own pace.

When children arrive at the program, they are given time to adjust. Children need not wait a long time for an activity to start. They are not rushed to finish an activity. Children rarely move in a large group or in a line.

When it is necessary for children to move as a group, the transition is smooth.

Staff clearly explain how the transition will happen. There is appropriate supervision during the transition to ensure that it will occur safely. There is a clear reason for needing to move as a group. Children are not forced to wait for a long time in silence.

NOTE:
Words that appear in **purple** are defined in the Glossary.

13. Children and youth can choose from a wide variety of activities.

There are regular opportunities for active, physical play.
Children have time indoors and outdoors for physical activity (e.g., a chance to dance, run, jump, climb, play active games and sports, and explore the environment).

There are regular opportunities for creative arts and dramatic play.
The program has a wide variety of arts and crafts materials: clay, paint, markers, beads, yarn for weaving and knitting, etc. There are costumes, puppets, and props on hand for dramatic play. Children have access to musical instruments and audio tapes.

There are regular opportunities for quiet activities and socializing.
Children can choose to sit and talk with friends or staff. They can choose to play quiet board games or help on a cooking project. They may decide to study alone, or just sit back and daydream.

Children have a chance to join enrichment activities that promote basic skills and higher-level thinking.
Children can work together on science projects. There are math games and materials to explore. Children can study the plants and animals that live in or around the building. They can create a newspaper, write a play, do homework, or use computers.

GUIDING QUESTIONS:

Do we have special-interest groups or clubs for older children?

Do activities help children learn new skills or explore interesting topics?

Can children become involved in long-term projects and productions?

ACTIVITIES

14. Activities reflect the mission of the program and promote the development of all the children and youth in the program.

GUIDING
QUESTIONS:

What is the mission of our program?

Who defined the mission? How is it shared with families, children, and staff?

How does the mission guide us in planning activities? How is our program different for 5- to 7-year-olds, 8- to 11-year-olds, and 11- to 14-year-olds?

Activities are in line with the styles, abilities, and interests of the individuals in the program.

Children are permitted to work at their own pace. Activities allow children to work alone, in pairs, or in large and small groups. Special tools are available to children who need help with fine motor skills (e.g. special scissors, thick pencils, and brushes). Quiet activities, such as storytelling, are adapted to include children who are more active.

Activities are well suited to the age range of children in the program.

Staff adapt projects to suit different age and interest levels. Projects for younger children can be completed within a week. Projects for older children may last eight to ten weeks. Physical games and sports offer varying levels of challenge to suit the players. Staff encourage expert children to help beginners learn a new skill.

Activities reflect the languages and cultures of the families served.

Staff involve children, families, and community members in planning activities. Food from a range of cultures is served for snack. Games from different cultures are played inside and outside. Folk tales and traditions from diverse groups provide the basis for plays, musical performances, art displays, and crafts projects.

Activities reflect and support the program's mission.
(See glossary for examples.)

15. There are sufficient materials to support program activities.

Materials are complete and in good repair.

Wooden equipment is free of splinters and rough edges. Hardware is not rusty or protruding. Board games and puzzles are in sturdy containers and have all their pieces. Balls are fully inflated. There is a wide variety of books in good condition.

There are enough materials for the number of children in the program.

Children rarely have to wait a long time to use materials, supplies, and equipment. A system is in place to help children share items in high demand (e.g., computers, pottery wheels, or new games). There are enough materials so that several activities can go on at the same time.

Materials are developmentally appropriate for the age range of the children in the program.

There are books for every reading ability. There are simple and more complex puzzles and board games (e.g., Candyland, Othello, Mancala, checkers and chess). There are computer games for young children as well as older youth. There are flexible materials that can be used in many ways (e.g., markers, stencils, paint, and clay). Many of the materials are adaptable for use by children with differing abilities.

Materials promote the program's mission.

(See glossary for examples.)

GUIDING QUESTIONS:

Are children able to find what they need to explore their interests and take part in activities?

Are some unable to participate because there aren't enough materials?

NOTE:
Words that appear in **purple** are defined in the Glossary.

SAFETY, HEALTH, & NUTRITION

SAFETY, HEALTH, & NUTRITION

16. The safety and security of children and youth are protected.

GUIDING
QUESTIONS:

Do families,
children, and
staff generally
feel that this is
a safe and
healthy envi-
ronment?

Have parents,
children, or
staff expressed
concern about
a potential
safety hazard?

Do we review
and discuss
future preven-
tion strategies?

There are no observable safety hazards in the program space.
All of the following are covered and secured: electrical cords,
heating pipes, sharp-edged objects. All stairs and climbing
structures have railings. The cubbies, shelves, and dividers
are secured so that they cannot tip over onto children.
Tables are stored in a safe manner so they will not fall on
anyone. The floor is free of dangerous clutter and spills.
The area is free of glass and other unsafe litter. The outdoor
play space is protected from traffic by fences or by other
means. Program entrance and exit areas are also sheltered
from traffic.

Systems are in place to protect the children from harm,
especially when they move from one place to another
or use the restroom.

There is appropriate supervision at all times. Children
know how to get help in situations where adults are not
directly supervising. A system is in place for monitoring
the location and arrival time of children who participate
in outside activities such as clubs, music lessons, and sports.
Devices such as intercoms, two-way radios and cordless
phones are used to make communication possible between
different areas within the program. A system is in place
to allow staff to know which children are in the bathroom
and how long they've been there. For example, children
may put a clothespin by their name and set an egg timer.
Access is monitored and staff respond when strangers
enter the program. For example, staff install a lock
or buzzer on doors.

Equipment for active play is safe.

Large equipment is bolted down. Swings are placed out of the way of passing children. All playground equipment is on a resilient surface (e.g., fine, loose sand, wood chips, or wood mulch about nine inches deep, or on rubber mats manufactured for such use). Children wear appropriate protective gear (e.g., helmets for biking, and helmets, wrist and knee guards for in-line skating).

A system is in place to keep unauthorized people from taking children from the program.

Staff know who is authorized to pick up each child. Staff know what to do if an unauthorized person attempts to pick up a child.

NOTE:
Words that appear in **purple** are defined in the Glossary.

SAFETY, HEALTH, & NUTRITION

17. The program provides an environment that protects and enhances the health of children and youth.

GUIDING
QUESTIONS:

**Do staff,
children,
or families
comment
on the
cleanliness of
the facility?**

**Have they
reported
concerns
about poten-
tial health
hazards?**

**How have
we responded
to these
concerns?**

The indoor and outdoor facilities are clean.

Floors, walls, and sinks are clean. Bad odors do not linger. Bathrooms are cleaned daily. Food service areas are disinfected after each use.

There are no observable health hazards in the indoor or outdoor space.

Children do not have unsupervised access to medicine, poisons, or cleaning agents such as bleach. Air quality in and around the facility is acceptable. Tap water is safe for drinking. Windows are secured.

There are adequate supplies and facilities for handwashing.

Signs or pictures are posted at each sink to show proper handwashing techniques. Soap dispensers are filled regularly. Towels are not shared.

The heat, ventilation, noise level, and light in the indoor space are comfortable.

Floor or table lamps are used when needed. The temperature can be turned up or down. Rugs and ceiling tiles are used to help absorb noise.

NOTE:
Words that
appear in **purple**
are defined in
the Glossary.

18. The program staff try to protect and enhance the health of children and youth.

Staff are responsive to the individual health needs of the children.

Staff are aware of the health needs of individual children. These needs may include dietary restrictions, allergies, and medication. Staff respect the confidentiality of children's health needs.

Staff protect children from communicable disease by separating children who become ill during the program.

There is a designated area to care for ill children. Staff follow the program's written policy when they respond to children who become ill.

Staff protect children from potential hazards such as the following: caustic or toxic art materials and cleaning agents, medications, and hot liquids; overexposure to heat or cold.

Toxic substances are kept in a locked cabinet, out of the reach of children. There is a sign-out form for any medication to be given to children. Directions for dosage are clearly marked and understood by staff. Staff closely supervise any activities that use hot liquids or heat-producing tools (e.g. boiling water, an iron, or stove). There is a supply of extra coats, gloves, and boots for winter. In summer, there is a shady outdoor space and access to water. Students stay indoors when the weather is bad.

Staff and children wash hands frequently, especially after using the toilet or before preparing food.

GUIDING QUESTIONS:

Do we wash our hands frequently? Why, or why not?

Do we make sure children wash their hands with soap and water?

Do we have a plan in place to care for a child who has become ill at the program?

How do we keep all staff informed of special health needs, such as allergies or asthma?

SAFETY, HEALTH, & NUTRITION

19. Children and youth are carefully supervised to maintain safety.

How do we
monitor
arrivals and
departures?

Do we take
attendance
immediately
and try to
find out
where absent
children are?

Does our
system enable
us to know
where children
are at all
times?

Do we know
which activi-
ties will need
extra super-
vision?

Are there high-
risk situations
that we should
try to avoid?

Staff note when children arrive, when they leave, and with whom they leave.

Staff use a checklist or other system to make note of absentees and late arrivals. A system is in place to inform staff that a child is leaving. Staff will permit only authorized people to pick up a child at the program. Staff are watchful of traffic risks during drop-off and pick-up times.

Staff know where the children are and what they are doing.

Staff move around an area so they can see all the children they are supervising. Staff position themselves in a way that allows them to watch as many children as possible. Staff know where children are during transitions (e.g., moving from outdoors to indoors, room to room, and using rest rooms). If children have permission to be out of sight, staff know where they are and will check on them at regular intervals.

Staff supervise children appropriately according to children's ages, abilities, and needs.

Staff give verbal and non-verbal signals to set clear limits for safety and behavior. Staff vary the level of supervision to match the needs of individuals and groups. Staff take children's temperaments and developmental stages into account in setting the level of supervision. Staff respect older children's need for independence.

Staff closely supervise activities that are potentially harmful.

Staff work with small, manageable groups when activities involve dangerous equipment (e.g., using carpentry tools, cooking, leatherworking). Staff closely watch children who are on climbing equipment. Staff watch out for traffic hazards when children are outdoors.

20. The program serves foods and drinks that meet the needs of children and youth.

The program serves healthy foods.

Foods high in fats, salts, and sugars are limited. Staff serve fruit juice and milk instead of fruit drinks and soda. A balance of fruits, vegetables, grains, and proteins is served. Snacks include healthy foods from various cultures.

Drinking water is readily available at all times.

Water from sinks and bubblers has been tested for quality. Filtered water is available at sites where the water quality is poor. Drinking water is carried along on off-site visits and field trips. Staff allow more time for children to drink water in hot weather.

The amount and type of food offered is appropriate for the ages and sizes of children.

The program offers serving sizes appropriate for children's ages and sizes. The program offers food to children who forget or bring only "junk food" from home. Staff support children's need to self-regulate the amount they eat. Most of the food put out at snack time gets eaten. Children do not complain a lot about disliking the food. They don't claim to be tired of having the same foods all the time. Options are provided for children with special dietary concerns (e.g., Kosher, vegetarian, and diabetic children).

Snacks and meals are timed appropriately for children.

Snacks are available for children when they arrive at the program. Children have enough time to eat without rushing. The timing is flexible enough to meet the needs of individuals. All children are notified before snacks are put away.

GUIDING QUESTIONS:

Do children enjoy eating the snacks we serve?

Do we involve them in planning or preparing snacks?

How do we respond to their requests for different snack foods?

Do we inform children and families about healthy nutrition?

NOTE:
Words that appear in **purple** are defined in the Glossary.

ADMINISTRATION

ADMINISTRATION

21. Staff/child ratios and group sizes permit the staff to meet the needs of children and youth.

GUIDING
QUESTIONS:

What are the staff-to-child ratios in our program?

How were the ratios determined? How are they enforced?

How do we modify the ratios based on the ages and needs of the children?

Do staff have time to interact with individual children and with small groups?

Staff/child ratios vary according to the ages and abilities of children. The ratio is between 1:10 and 1:15 for groups of children age six and older. The ratio is between 1:8 and 1:12 for groups that include children under age six.

Kindergarten groups tend to have more staff than older or multi-age groups. Ratios are sometimes lower when staff are working with children with special needs. In groups where more adults are present, the children receive additional guidance and support. The adults are able to be more responsive, and can nurture relationships between children and staff. Volunteers are not included in the staff/child ratios unless they meet staff qualifications and regularly take part in the program.

Staff/child ratios and group sizes vary according to the type and complexity of the activity, but group sizes do not exceed 30.

Ratios and group sizes are smaller when children are learning a new or difficult skill. This is also true for projects that use potentially dangerous equipment (e.g., cooking or carpentry). Group sizes tend to be larger with sports, art activities, reading, or quiet board games. The ratios are low enough so that staff have time to talk with individual children and help them be successful in activities.

There is a plan to provide adequate staff coverage in case of emergencies.

A child in need of medical care is always accompanied by a staff member. During such emergencies, a suitable number of adults are on hand to remain with the other children. If a staff member becomes ill during program time, there are still enough staff to care for the children. If one staff member is sufficient to meet child-to-staff ratios, a second adult is on hand to assist in case emergencies occur.

Substitute staff are used to maintain ratios when regular staff are absent.

The program keeps an up-to-date list of adults who are qualified to serve as substitutes. The responsibilities and procedures for substitutes are defined and carried out. Substitutes are evaluated by staff and directors.

NOTE:
Words that appear in **purple** are defined in the Glossary.

ADMINISTRATION

22. Children and youth are supervised at all times.

GUIDING
QUESTIONS:

**Are we happy
with our
system for
supervising
arrivals and
departures?
How can we
hope to know
what children
are doing at
all times?**

**Do staff
who super-
vise certain
activities, such
as sledding
and swim-
ming, receive
special train-
ing?**

**Can we
improve our
system of
supervision?**

Children's arrivals are supervised.

Staff know when children are expected to arrive. Staff have a quick system to check on late arrivals or absences. When questions arise, staff contact the school or a responsible adult listed on emergency forms. Staff do not rely on children to report or confirm other children's absences.

Children's departures are supervised.

Children depart according to the written instructions of the families (e.g., who is allowed to pick up a child, whether a child can walk home, etc.). Staff keep written records to show who picked up a child.

Staff have a system for knowing where the children are at all times.

Staff have a system for knowing where the children are as they move from room to room, or from inside to outside. A plan is in place for handling missing or lost children. The program has a policy that allows older children more independence. The policy is worked out with the children, their families, and the staff.

Staff plan for different levels of supervision according to the level of risk involved in an activity.

A written plan is in place for providing increased supervision for certain activities (e.g., carpentry, cooking, swimming, biking, sledding, ice skating, rollerblading, etc.). Staff who supervise these activities receive specialized training, as determined by industry safety standards. Extra adults are present on field trips that are difficult to supervise (e.g., trips to amusement parks, beaches, ski areas, campgrounds, etc.).

NOTE:
Words that
appear in **purple**
are defined in
the Glossary.

23. Staff support families' involvement in the program.

There is a policy that allows family members to visit any time throughout the day.
> Staff welcome families to the program whenever they visit. When possible, staff interact with visiting family members. Staff use newsletters and phone calls to remind parents that they are welcome to "drop in."

Staff offer orientation sessions for new families.
> Staff set aside time to tell new families all about the program. When a child moves into a different part of the program (e.g., the summer program or a special program for youth), staff meet with families to discuss the change. Whenever possible, staff offer orientation sessions in the home language of the families. Each family gets a copy of written policies, including the program's hours of operation, fees, subsidies, illness policy, etc. This document also states the program's mission and philosophy. Written material is translated for families who do not speak or read the majority language. As much as possible, pictographs are used to convey written information to non-readers. Adult interpreters are available when needed.

Staff keep families informed about the program.
> Staff send home notices and newsletters about program activities and events. Whenever possible, this information is written in the family's home language. Staff follow up written notices with phone calls or personal contact. There is a bulletin board that displays information for parents. Notices are written in the languages of the families in the program.

Key 23
continued next page

continued next page

GUIDING QUESTIONS:

What systems do we have in place to support family involvement?

Are there other things we could try?

How will increased family involvement make our program stronger?

Can we find a way to include more of the families who haven't participated regularly in the past?

Can we see a pattern that shows us which families may be getting left out?

23. Staff support families' involvement in the program.

Key 23
continued from previous page

Staff encourage families to give input and to get involved in program events.

Staff ask families to comment on the program via notes, surveys, and parent meetings. The program's advisory board includes a number of parents. Staff urge families to share their skills, hobbies, or family traditions. Staff invite family members to special events (e.g., plays, field trips, and picnics). Staff respect different cultural styles and try a variety of ways to involve families (e.g., meetings are held in the home language of the families.). The program may arrange transportation for special events and meetings.

NOTE:
Words that appear in **purple** are defined in the Glossary.

24. Staff, families, and schools share important information to support the well-being of children and youth.

Program policies require that staff and family members communicate about the child's well-being.

Parents or guardians answer questions about a child's background and history. Families keep staff informed of any major changes at home or at school. Staff inform families in writing about injuries, accidents, illnesses, etc. Staff are happy to speak with parents or guardians about their children's experiences in the program. The program makes provisions for families who do not speak or read the majority language.

Staff, families, and schools work together as a team to set goals for each child; they work with outside specialists when necessary.

Staff and families meet to discuss a child's behavior, health, friendships, accomplishments, etc. When a child is known to have special needs, staff meet with teachers, families, and outside experts. Staff make an effort to support the goals set by a child's Special Education Team. Staff work closely with other adults to provide consistency for children with behavior issues. Staff consult specialists to learn how best to help children with diverse physical abilities and disabilities. Staff seek advice from doctors and nurses about medical issues.

Key 24
continued next page

What steps can we take to find out more about our children? How does sharing information help us better serve our children?

What policies are in place for contacting schools? Where are these policies documented?

Do we know what other programs are doing to form these links? How can we learn from them?

ADMINISTRATION

Key 24
*continued from
previous page*

24. Staff, families, and schools share important information to support the well-being of children and youth.

Staff and families share information about how to support children's development.

Staff and families discuss any concerns about a child's development. Children are often included in these discussions. The program arranges for experts to speak on a variety of topics (e.g., nutrition, child development, conflict resolution, etc.). Families are invited to attend these sessions. Staff help parents form groups to discuss topics of interest to families. Staff and families meet to define policies for handling sensitive topics (e.g., violence, racism, sexuality, substance abuse, etc.). Staff maintain a parent library of relevant books and articles. Staff inform families about timely opportunities (e.g., childcare subsidies, medical, counseling, and career services).

Staff and families join together to communicate and work with the schools.

Staff keep informed about special school projects and events. Staff encourage children to be motivated and successful in school. Staff help with homework and value children's academic efforts. Staff are eager to talk with teachers about ways to help children achieve. Staff meet with families and school personnel in order to help the school gain a sense of the whole child.

NOTE:
Words that appear in **purple** are defined in the Glossary.

25. The program builds links to the community.

Staff provide information about community resources to meet the needs of children and their families.

Bulletin boards and newsletters contain information about upcoming community events (e.g., free dental screenings, fire-prevention seminars, and parenting classes). When needed, staff are able to refer families to local agencies (e.g., health clinics, food programs, counseling services, language classes, crisis intervention, etc.).

The program develops a list of community resources. The staff draw from these resources to expand program offerings.

Staff ask families for ideas in developing resources that reflect the home language and culture. Resources are well suited to the needs of children in the program (e.g., health, culture, language, learning styles, etc.). Staff use the list when planning field trips and inviting special guests.

The staff plan activities to help children get to know the larger community.

Children have a chance to attend outings and field trips (e.g., walking tours, parks, museums, performances, and cultural events). The program hosts visitors and special events from the community. Children have an opportunity to join local groups and teams (e.g., sports, drama, music). Children have an opportunity to meet adult coaches and mentors from the community.

The program offers community-service options, especially for older children.

Children are encouraged to take part in community projects (e.g., recycling, park cleanups, fund-raising events, etc.). Children are able to volunteer for projects that benefit younger children, senior citizens, children's hospitals and local shelters. Children organize food and clothing collection for local agencies.

GUIDING QUESTIONS:

How can we expand what we offer beyond the walls of our program?

Are children aware of the resources in our community?

Do children feel part of the larger community?

How do we give children a chance to provide community service?

ADMINISTRATION

26. The program's indoor space meets the needs of staff.

There is enough room in the indoor space for staff to plan various program activities.

GUIDING QUESTIONS:

Is there enough room for all the activities we plan?

Do we have adequate and convenient storage?

Does lack of space or storage ever limit the activities we provide?

Is a system in place to regularly maintain the facility and respond to the changing needs of our program?

When indoor space is used for active play (e.g., dance, aerobics, or basketball) there are 75 square feet per child. There are 35 square feet per child for quiet activities such as homework, reading, or holding club meetings. There are 45 square feet per child for small group and enrichment activities such as woodworking, arts and crafts, and science experiments.

Staff have access to adequate and convenient storage.

Staff rarely have to carry heavy equipment long distances or large amounts of materials for set-up and clean-up. The amount or location of storage does not limit the activities staff can offer. Staff have a place to store personal belongings. Programs in shared space have portable equipment on wheels.

The indoor space meets or exceeds local health and safety codes.

The space has passed health, building, and fire inspections. To be sure codes are met, the program has arranged its own inspection of the program space by a qualified person. The indoor space is barrier free and accessible to people using wheelchairs or walkers. Someone is routinely responsible to check that entrances and exits are unobstructed and well lit. This person also makes sure that surfaces are washed and sanitized.

Written guidelines are in place regarding the use and maintenance of the program facility.

Staff know whom to call for repairs on heating, plumbing, or telephone systems. In programs with shared space, a written policy spells out the use of space, supplies, equipment, and methods of communication. Guidelines note each group's responsibility for cleaning, maintenance, and routine costs (e.g., utilities, insurance, and repairs). Sharing of the program space does not interfere with program activities. Program plans are seldom superseded by other groups (e.g., youth groups, choir, sports teams).

NOTE:
Words that appear in **purple** are defined in the Glossary.

ADMINISTRATION

27. The outdoor space is large enough to meet the needs of children, youth, and staff.

GUIDING
QUESTIONS:

**Do we
provide as
many outdoor
activities as
the children
would like?**

**Does the size,
type, or condi-
tion of our
outdoor space
limit the
variety of
activities we
can offer?**

**Who is
responsible for
maintaining
the play-
ground?**

**How can we
maximize our
program's
offerings by
making better
use of
surrounding
outdoor areas?**

There is enough room in the outdoor space for all program activities.

> If the program does not have its own outdoor space, it has daily access to an off-site space such as a park or playground. If the program has a small space, children's outdoor time is staggered so that children are not crowded.

The outdoor space meets or exceeds local health and safety codes.

> Clean drinking water is available outdoors. Access to restrooms is restricted to prevent public use. Fencing is provided when needed to ensure the safety of children.

Staff use outdoor areas to provide new outdoor play experiences.

> Groups take walks in the neighborhood or visit local spots for exploring nature (e.g., creeks, ponds, beaches, and forests). Staff take children on trips to a baseball field, swimming pool, or skating rink, if possible.

There is a procedure in place for regularly checking the safety and maintenance of the outdoor play space.

> Someone is routinely responsible for making sure the sidewalks are free of ice, snow, and slippery mud. Someone routinely tests to be sure that large equipment is anchored and in good repair (e.g., free of rust, splinters, or loose nails and screws).

28. Staff, children, and youth work together to plan and implement suitable activities, which are consistent with the program's philosophy.

Staff ask children to share their ideas for planning so that activities will reflect children's interests.

> Staff regularly involve children in planning for snack, daily activities, and special events. Staff ask children to help select new materials, supplies, and equipment. Staff plan activities that reflect the cultures of children (e.g. music, dance, stories, feasts).

The program's daily activities are in line with its mission and philosophy.

> The schedule and activity choices allow children to participate in activities that reflect the mission and philosophy.

Staff keep on file their records of activity planning.

> Written plans with clearly stated goals are available to staff and substitutes. Staff jot down notes about an activity's success so future staff can learn from past experiences. Written plans are used to assess the needs and interests of children.

Staff plan activities that will reflect the cultures of the families in the program and the broad diversity of human experience.

> Staff regularly choose materials that reflect the language, music, stories, games, and crafts from various cultural traditions. Staff invite children and families to share recipes, songs, stories, and photos that represent their culture and experiences. Staff avoid using a "tourist" approach to studying different cultures. Muticultural activities occur throughout the year, rather than only during holidays.

GUIDING QUESTIONS:

What systems are in place to include children when planning activities?

How do we document activities in a way that helps us plan for the future and learn from the past?

NOTE: Words that appear in *purple* are defined in the Glossary.

ADMINISTRATION

29. Program policies and procedures are in place to protect the safety of the children and youth.

GUIDING
QUESTIONS:

Under what circumstances might we need to close our program?

Is a plan in place to handle this situation?

What do we do when we notice a situation that might be dangerous?

What can we do to help children and staff respond effectively?

Staff and children know what to do in case of general emergency.

Emergency procedures for exiting during a fire are posted and practiced regularly. Staff check smoke detectors and fire extinguishers every three months. Fire extinguishers are visible and accessible. Staff know how to use fire extinguishers. Staff and families know what to do in emergency situations (e.g., in case of fire, earthquake, tornado, snowstorm, etc.). Staff are prepared to respond when strangers attempt to intrude or disrupt the program.

The program has established procedures to prevent accidents and manage emergencies.

Staff are expected to be alert to safety hazards (e.g., litter or glass, equipment that has become unbolted or rusted). Staff take action to correct safety hazards. There are specific procedures for higher risk activities (e.g., swimming, gymnastics, sledding, etc.) Staff are trained to handle incidents involving poison, burns, and other medical emergencies.

The program has established policies to transport children safely; it complies with all legal requirements for vehicles and drivers.

All cars, vans, buses, or taxis used for transporting children on field trips or to and from school are licensed, inspected, and maintained. All drivers of vehicles used to transport children are adequately trained and licensed. The program checks to be sure all drivers have good driving records.

A system is in place to prevent unauthorized people from taking children from the program.

Staff know who is allowed to pick up each child. Staff know what to do if an unauthorized person attempts to pick up a child.

ADMINISTRATION

30. Program policies exist to protect and enhance the health of all children and youth.

GUIDING
QUESTIONS:

What policies
are in place
regarding the
health of
children in
the program?

Do we have
policies in place
to prevent or
address sus-
pected cases
of child abuse?

What steps
do we take
to document
these policies
and train staff
to implement
them?

There is current documentation showing that the program has met the state and/or local health and safety guidelines and/or regulations.

The program's license is posted. Inspection reports are kept on file. Written plans document a program's efforts to remain in compliance with all local health and safety codes.

There are written policies and procedures to ensure the health and safety of children.

The program has a handbook that describes procedures for the following:

- administering medications,
- controlling communicable diseases,
- responding to sick children,
- dealing with children who have chronic health conditions such as allergies,
- protecting children from toxic materials,
- administering first aid,
- handling medical emergencies,
- responding to natural disasters,
- reporting suspected child abuse or neglect,
- dealing with inebriated parents.

No smoking is allowed in the program.

A no-smoking policy is enforced at all times. The policy applies to both the indoor and outdoor spaces, as well as field trips. The staff and parent handbooks clearly state the no-smoking policy. No smoking signs are posted. Staff cigarettes are never visible to the children.

Staff are always prepared to respond to accidents and emergencies.

A staff person trained in first aid and CPR is available at all times. During program hours, a telephone is always accessible for incoming and outgoing calls. Written emergency numbers (e.g., for police, fire, ambulance, poison control) are posted near the phone. Emergency information about the children is taken on field trips. Families are contacted immediately in case of emergency. A first-aid kit is available at all times. Staff receive blood-born pathogen training.

NOTE: Words that appear in **purple** are defined in the Glossary.

ADMINISTRATION

31. All staff are professionally qualified to work with children and youth.

GUIDING
QUESTIONS:

**What training
opportunities
do we offer
new and
continuing
staff?**

**How are staff
made aware
of training
opportunities?**

**How does
the type of
training differ
according to
the person's
role or level
of responsi-
bility at the
program?**

31a Staff meet the requirements for experience with school-age children in recreational settings.
(See Appendix.)

31b Staff have received the recommended type and amount of preparation. They meet the requirements that are specific to school-age child care and relevant to their particular jobs.
(See Appendix.)

31c Staff meet minimum age requirements.
(See Appendix.)

31d Enough qualified staff are in place to meet all levels of responsibility. Qualified staff are hired in all areas: to administer the program, to oversee its daily operations, and to supervise children.
(See Appendix.)

NOTE:
Words that
appear in **purple**
are defined in
the Glossary.

32. Staff (paid, volunteer, and substitute) are given an orientation to the job before working with children and youth.

A written job description that outlines responsibilities to children, families, and the program is reviewed with each staff member.

> The job description includes expectations regarding space set-up, activity planning, supervision, and behavior management.

Written personnel policies are reviewed with staff.

> Staff can read and ask questions about their hours (e.g., schedules, breaks, time for planning and training). Benefits and grievance procedures are clearly spelled out.

Written program policies and procedures, including emergency procedures and confidentiality policies, are reviewed with staff.

> New staff can read about program policies and refer to written descriptions at a later date. They can also hear these policies described by the director or another well-informed staff member. Basic ethical standards are reviewed with all new staff (e.g., the need for confidentiality about information on children, families, and other staff).

New staff are given a comprehensive orientation to the program philosophy, routines, and practices. They are personally introduced to the people with whom they will be working.

> New staff are introduced to the custodian, school principal, agency director, as well as co-workers in the program. They are given a tour of the program space and shown where to find materials and supplies. They are told about the schedule, activities, guidance policies, and the special needs of individual children. They have a chance to discuss any questions they may have about the program's mission and philosophy.

GUIDING QUESTIONS:

Have we surveyed staff about what they wish they had known when they started?

Do we find ways to evaluate the orientation in order to improve it?

How can we incorporate staff's ideas in future training?

ADMINISTRATION

GUIDING
QUESTIONS:

How do we
assess the
training needs
of staff? What
methods do
we use to
train staff?

How do we
evaluate the
staff training
we provide?

Do non-
English-speak-
ing staff have
the same
opportunity
for professional
growth as their
English-speak-
ing peers?

How can we
do a better job
of providing
training and
professional
growth oppor-
tunities for
all our staff?

33. The training needs of the staff are assessed, and training is relevant to the responsibilities of each job. Assistant Group Leaders receive at least 15 hours of training annually. Group Leaders receive at least 18 hours of training annually. Senior Group Leaders receive at least 21 hours of training annually. Site Directors receive at least 24 hours of training annually. Program Administrators receive at least 30 hours of training annually. *(See Appendix)*

Staff receive training in how to work with families and how to relate to children in ways that promote their development.

This training includes:

- how to foster children's self-esteem.

- positive techniques for guiding children's behavior and for helping children to guide their own behavior.

- responding to the differing needs of children (e.g., according to age, temperament, culture, and special abilities).

- anti-bias training and how to apply it in working with children and families.

- problem solving, conflict resolution, and development of respect for peers.

- how to foster a sense of community among the children and staff (e.g., trust building).

- how to help children improve academic skills, especially reading, writing, and math. (This training is critical for staff who will be helping with homework, tutoring, and remediation.)

- positive techniques for communicating with families. This should include learning the languages and cultural traditions of the families in the program.

- learning about different types of families (e.g., single-parent, dual-career, blended, adoptive, gay and lesbian, etc.).

Program directors and administrators receive training in program management and staff supervision.

Training addresses the following: cultural issues, financial management, risk management, quality assurance, and staff supervision. Program directors and administrators have a chance to visit other programs and share best practices with their peers. Directors and administrators have access to supervisory and management books and magazines.

Staff receive training in how to set up program space and design activities to support program goals.

Staff learn how to use mobile furniture and equipment to create interest areas in large, open, shared space. Staff learn how to adapt space and activities for children with disabilities. They learn how to supervise games and sports, including non-competitive, team-building activities. Staff learn how to work with older children to develop clubs and hobbies that will hold older children's' interest.

Staff receive training in how to promote the safety, health, and nutrition of children.

Staff are trained in first aid and rescue breathing. Staff know how to identify, document, and report cases of suspected child abuse and neglect. Staff understand the nutritional needs of school-age children. They know how to prepare healthy meals and snacks under sanitary conditions.

NOTE: Words that appear in **purple** are defined in the Glossary.

ADMINISTRATION

34. Staff receive appropriate support to make their work experience positive.

The program has a plan in place to offer the best possible wages and working conditions in an effort to reduce staff turnover.

GUIDING
QUESTIONS:

How is the morale of those of us who work here?

Is a plan in place to review our compensation and benefits package?

Can we go to our peers and supervisor for support on tough issues?

Do we feel that our work is valued by the program director, the families, and our peers?

Compensation takes education and experience into account. Staff are compensated for time spent in training and planning. Wages are above the minimum hourly wage and are competitive with other human services jobs.

Full-time staff receive benefits, including health insurance and paid leaves of absence. Staff are also given paid breaks and paid preparation time.

If possible, the program provides the following: dental, life, and disability insurance; retirement benefits; and subsidized child care.

Staff are given ample time to discuss their own concerns regarding the program.

Staff meet regularly (for at least an hour, twice a month) to discuss program operations and the changing needs of children. Staff are able to communicate daily about issues that need immediate attention (e.g., family crises, behavior issues, changes in dietary or medical needs). Staff discuss new strategies for rough transitions. Staff develop a plan for responding consistently to a child who is having problems. Staff plan program-wide activities and get-togethers. Staff have a process for negotiating interpersonal differences (e.g., cultural, gender, or value differences).

Staff receive continuous supervision and feedback. This includes written performance reviews on a timely basis.

Supervisor and staff member regularly discuss activities and interactions with children. They work together to set goals for the coming month. Each staff person receives a written evaluation at least yearly. These evaluations include comments based on observation of staff performance. Staff participate in their own assessment. The program keeps written, updated notes on staff performance and feedback. It keeps records on file of staff participation in continuing education and training.

NOTE:
Words that appear in **purple** are defined in the Glossary.

ADMINISTRATION

35. The administration provides sound management of the program.

GUIDING
QUESTIONS:

**Do we have
a long term
strategy to
keep our
program
sound?**

**Are budget
projections
part of our
strategic
planning?**

**What do
we do to
make sure
our program
is stable,
high quality
and meets
the needs
of children,
families,
and staff?**

The financial management of the program supports the program's goals.

The program develops an annual budget that reflects the program's priorities. Income and expenses are reviewed quarterly. The financial plan includes budgets for payroll, staff development, activities, materials, supplies, equipment, and food. Program staff have a chance to help with budget planning. The program seeks outside funds to support the financial plan (e.g., subsidies, public and private support, a strong marketing plan). The program has adequate auto and liability insurance.

The administration oversees the recruitment and retention of program staff.

Affirmative action practices are implemented. The program obtains positive and professional references about all staff and volunteers before they begin to work with children. Written references or notes from telephone conversations are kept in personnel files. A criminal record check is done. The director examines recurring reasons for staff turnover and takes all possible action to reduce unnecessary turnover.

The director involves staff, board, families, and children in both long-term planning and daily decision-making.

The director provides support (e.g., orientation, training, and information) to help the board of directors or advisory group to make informed decisions. The director communicates frequently, both formally and informally, with the program host, agency executive director, and schools.

Administrators assist with ongoing evaluation. They aim for improvement in all areas of the program.

Parents, staff, and children are involved in evaluating the program. A program assessment or evaluation is conducted at least once a year (using, for example, surveys, focus groups, or observations). Findings are shared with everyone in the program community. Based on the results of the evaluation, a program improvement plan is developed. The plan includes goals, action steps, a timetable, and resources. Staff work on these goals to improve the program.

NOTE:
Words that appear in **purple** are defined in the Glossary.

ADMINISTRATION

GUIDING
QUESTIONS:

Does our
mission
statement
clearly reflect
our program's
philosophy
and goals?

Have we found
the best ways
to make our
program
affordable to
all families?

How can we do
a better job of
responding to
the needs of
children and
families in our
community?

What policies
exist to make
our program
accessible to
children with
special needs?

36. Program policies and procedures are responsive to the needs of children, youth, and families in the community.

A written mission statement sets forth the program's philosophy and goals.

The philosophy clarifies the program's primary purposes (e.g., supervision, recreation, socialization, academic support, family support). The philosophy guides decisions about staffing, curriculum, and policy.

The program makes itself affordable to all families by using all possible community resources and sources of subsidy.

Sliding fees, state and federal subsidies, and scholarships are used to make the program affordable. Eligible families receive easy-to-read information about program fees, subsidies, and childcare tax credit. This information is available in the family's home language.

The program's hours of operation are based on families' needs.

The program asks families what hours and days they need childcare. The program makes a reasonable effort to provide care when families need it. This often includes before-school care and extended hours on holidays and school vacations.

It is the program's policy to enroll children with special needs.

The program adapts space and activities so that all children can participate fully. Program staff are knowledgeable about the Americans for Disabilities Act. They use it to make decisions about serving children with special needs.

NEXT STEPS

C reating the best possible experience for children and youth is a daily challenge. The NAA Standards and the Guiding Questions are designed to help you discuss your program's strengths and to identify areas where you'd like to make improvements. Striving towards excellence is a gradual, developmental process—one which is best approached in stages.

After you have become familiar with the Keys, Standards, and Guiding Questions, the next step in the process of program improvement is to do a more in-depth self-study. During the self-study, program staff will involve children, families, and other decision-makers in their discussions. The self-study leads to an action plan and to long lasting and fundamental program improvement. It may also lead to the decision to apply for NAA Accreditation.

The following questions will help you decide whether your program is ready to make the investment in taking this next step. They are based on what we learned from the experiences of programs in the "Pilot" phase of the Program Improvement and Accreditation System. Many of these indicators of readiness were formulated by Susan O'Connor, formerly from the National Institute on Out-of-School Time (formerly the SACC Project).

If you can answer "yes" to four out of five of these questions in each category, you are probably ready to embark on a full self-study using *ASQ: Advancing School-Age Child Care Quality*. This tool is located in the NAA Accreditation Package.

If you answer "no" to two or more in each group of the questions below, here are some ways that you can seek help to increase support for your program.

■ Visit another school-age childcare program. Invite other school-age care staff to visit your program. Get together with other school-age care directors and staff to discuss how to build these program supports.

■ Take this book of standards and the following questions to the head of your agency or the principal of your school to get their advice on how you can get to "yes."

■ Find out who offers school-age care training in your community: for example, the local resource and referral agency, a community college, your NAA affiliate, or the National Institute on Out-of-School Time.

■ Attend workshops, training events, and conferences. Look for people who would be good advisors or consultants to come to your program. In the meantime, continue to discuss the Guiding Questions in the Standards and try ways to meet them one key at a time.

■ Order the self-study and accredition materials from NAA and use parts of the ASQ manual to start working on program improvements.

Administrative Support

	YES	UNSURE	NO
1. Will our director be able to spend at least 10 hours a month coordinating the self-study and the action plan?	❏	❏	❏
2. Does our program's administration support us in doing this?	❏	❏	❏
3. Will we have a budget to support our action plan?	❏	❏	❏
4. Will our staff have time (at least three hours a month) to talk about the self-study and action plan?	❏	❏	❏
5. Will we be able to get 20 hours of EXTRA clerical help this year to do the paperwork?	❏	❏	❏

Forming the Self-Study (ASQ) Team

	YES	UNSURE	NO
1. Does our director want to facilitate a self-study team with staff, family members, and others?	❏	❏	❏
2. Will at least two of our staff be able to be on the team and attend meetings outside of the program hours?	❏	❏	❏
3. Do we have families who would be willing to spend about 15 hours this year to be on the self-study team?	❏	❏	❏
4. Does someone from our program's administration want to be on the self-study team?	❏	❏	❏
5. Will we be able to ask someone from the children's school to be part of our self-study team?	❏	❏	❏

Program Stability

	YES	UNSURE	NO
1. Has our director been working with the program for at least six months? Do we expect to have the same director for the next year?	❏	❏	❏
2. Have our site coordinator and/or senior group leader been here for at least three months? Do we expect to have the same site coordinator and/or senior group leader for the next year?	❏	❏	❏
3. Are we in the same facility as last year? Will we be in the same facility for the next year?	❏	❏	❏
4. Will our enrollment increase be less than 25% in the next year?	❏	❏	❏
5. Do we have substitutes for staff?	❏	❏	❏

If you answered "no" or "unsure" to some of the questions in this section, please refer to Keys 34 and 35 in the Standards. These sections will help guide your strategy for greater program stability.

| | YES | UNSURE | NO |

Staff Development

1. Do we have an orientation for new staff? ❑ ❑ ❑

2. Do all of our staff have first-aid training? ❑ ❑ ❑

3. Do we provide at least 10 hours of in-service training for all of our staff each year? ❑ ❑ ❑

4. Do our staff attend professional meetings or training conferences? ❑ ❑ ❑

5. Does our director belong to a director's support group or a professional organization, such as NAA? ❑ ❑ ❑

If you answered "no" or "unsure" to some of the questions in this section, please refer to Keys 31, 32, and 33 in the Standards. These sections will help guide your staff development strategies.

Family Involvement

1. Do we always greet family members when they drop off or pick up the children? Do we talk to every family about once a week? ❑ ❑ ❑

2. Do we have a bulletin board or a newsletter for families? ❑ ❑ ❑

3. Do we have family events like potluck suppers or performances by the children? ❑ ❑ ❑

4. Do family members volunteer to help our program? ❑ ❑ ❑

5. Do we have a parent advisory group or parents on our governing board? ❑ ❑ ❑

If you answered "no" or "unsure" to some of the questions in this section, please refer to Keys 7, 23, and 24 in the Standards. These sections will help guide your program improvement strategies for more successful family involvement.

Program Policies

1. Do we have a written mission statement? ❑ ❑ ❑

2. Do we have written job descriptions and personnel policies? ❑ ❑ ❑

3. Do we have written staff guidelines including health and safety procedures? ❑ ❑ ❑

4. Do we have a parent handbook? ❑ ❑ ❑

5. Is our ratio at least 1:15 for children ages six to 13 and at least 1:12 for groups with children under age six? ❏ ❏ ❏

If you answered "no" or "unsure" to some of the questions in this section, please refer to Keys 14, 21, 23, 29, 30, and 32 in the Standards. These sections will help guide you in developing successful program policies.

Shared Decision-Making

1. Does our director encourage staff to contribute new ideas and help make decisions? ❏ ❏ ❏

2. Do we ask families for their opinions and ideas? ❏ ❏ ❏

3. Do the children in our program help us decide on program plans? ❏ ❏ ❏

4. Are we willing to have parents, other staff, and community members observe our program? ❏ ❏ ❏

5. Do we believe that listening to families, the children, community members, and each other will lead to better decisions about the program? ❏ ❏ ❏

If you answered "no" or "unsure" to some of the questions in this section, please refer to Keys 23, 24, 25, 28, 35, and 36 in the Standards. These sections will help guide your strategy for shared decision-making.

The NAA Quality Pyramid

Activities

Indoor *Outdoor*
Environment

Safety, Health, and Nutrition

Child/Child *Staff/Child*
Human Relationships
Staff/Staff *Staff/Family*

**Program Organization, Procedures, Policies
The "Infrastructure" of Quality**

NAA Program Improvement and Accreditation
Steps in the Process

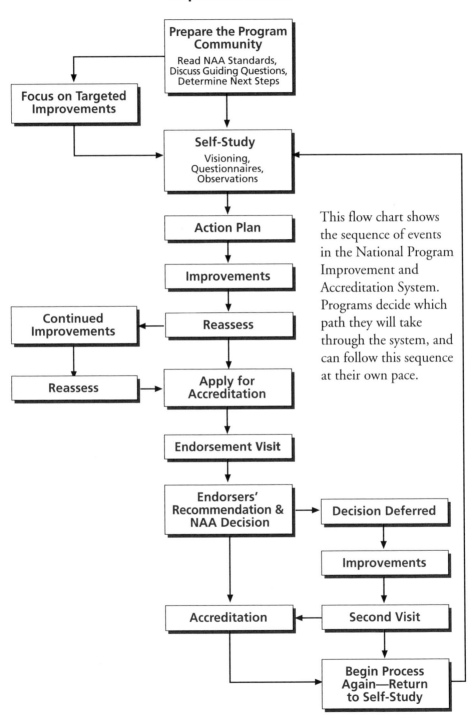

Prepare the Program Community
Read NAA Standards, Discuss Guiding Questions, Determine Next Steps

Focus on Targeted Improvements

Self-Study
Visioning, Questionnaires, Observations

Action Plan

Improvements

Continued Improvements

Reassess

Reassess

Apply for Accreditation

Endorsement Visit

Endorsers' Recommendation & NAA Decision

Decision Deferred

Improvements

Accreditation

Second Visit

Begin Process Again—Return to Self-Study

This flow chart shows the sequence of events in the National Program Improvement and Accreditation System. Programs decide which path they will take through the system, and can follow this sequence at their own pace.

How are the Standards used for accreditation?

These Standards are the basis of the self-study process and of accreditation. Programs will rate themselves using these tools to make an improvement plan. Endorsers will rate the programs on these Standards when they apply for accreditation.

The ratings are done on a four point scale:

0 = Standard not met (You're not doing this at all. You need to develop a plan to meet this Standard.)

1 = Standard somewhat met (You're beginning to meet this Standard, but there's still much more that you could be doing.)

2 = Standard substantially met (You're doing this more often than not. There is still some room for improvement.)

3 = Standard fully met (You're consistently meeting this Standard. Excellent!)

Will programs have to get a "3" on every Standard to be accredited?

Definitely not! Accreditation will mean that a program is in substantial compliance with the Standards overall. There may be some Standards that you meet more completely than others. However, in order to become accredited, programs must meet the Standards related to human relationships, health and safety, and ratios. These Standards will not be waived, and programs must receive a rating of no less than "2" in order to be accredited. The NAA Accreditation decision will be based on the overall quality of the experience you provide for the children in your program, as well as your ratings on individual Standards.

NAA is dedicated to supporting you in your work of providing quality care for children and youth in their out-of-school time.

This section of the Standards was designed to give you an overview of the system as a whole. You can decide:

- how you want to work on meeting the Standards,
- if and when you choose to begin a complete self-study, and
- if and when you choose to pursue accreditation.

All of the materials in the Program Improvement and Accreditation System are designed to help you improve the quality of your program and achieve your program's mission, regardless of whether you choose to pursue NAA Accreditation.

Appendix One
Staff Qualifications

T he following chart outlines the staff roles needed for effective program operation. We realize that the job titles your program uses may vary slightly from the titles we've listed here. Please choose the job description that most closely matches the job title in your program. Some programs may not have all of the positions listed below. Every program must have at least one person who is a qualified Administrator. If there are more than thirty children in your program, there must also be one staff member who is qualified as a Senior Group Leader.

We also realize that in some programs, one staff person may assume the responsibilities of more than one position. When this happens, the person must have the qualifications required for the highest level of responsibility. For example:

In a single site program, the same person may act as both the Program Administrator and the Site Director. In that case this person must meet the qualifications for the Program Administrator. If the same person acts as both Site Director and Senior Group Leader, she would need to meet the qualifications of Site Director. **The titles used in programs vary, so the responsibility assumed by that staff member will determine the qualifications required.**

LEVELS OF RESPONSIBILITY

Program Administrator	Overall direction of the program ■ developing a mission, goals, and policies for the program ■ program implementation and evaluation ■ administration, including fiscal management ■ organizational development, including management of human resources
Site Director	Daily operations of the program ■ supervising staff ■ communicating with families ■ building relationships with the host community ■ overseeing all program activities
Senior Group Leader	Supervision and guidance of children in the program ■ program planning ■ communicating with families ■ supervising support staff ■ relating to the community
Group Leader	Supervision and guidance of children in the program under the direction of a Senior Group Leader ■ same as the Senior Group Leader
Assistant Group Leader	Supervision and guidance of children under the direct supervision of a Group Leader

MINIMUM QUALIFICATIONS

Position	Experience	Education	Professional Preparation
Program Administrator	One year	Associate's or Bachelor's Degree in Related Field	Six credit hours: ■ child and youth development (3) ■ administration (3)
		——*or*——	
	Two years	Bachelor's Degree in Unrelated Field	Twelve credit hours: ■ child and youth development (3) ■ administration (3) ■ other areas related to sac programming (6)

Position	Experience	Education	Professional Preparation
Site Director	Six months	Bachelor's Degree in Related Field	Six credit hours: ■ child and youth development (3) ■ other areas related to sac programming (3)
		——*or*——	
	One year	Bachelor's Degree in Unrelated Field	Nine credit hours: ■ child and youth development (3) ■ other areas related to sac programming (6)
		——*or*——	
	Eighteen months	AA Degree or two years of college in a related field or equivalent certification	Nine credit hours: ■ child and youth development (3) ■ other areas related to sac programming (6)
Senior Group Leader		Bachelor's Degree in related field	
		——*or*——	
	Three months	Bachelor's Degree in unrelated field	Six credit hours: ■ child and youth development (3) ■ other areas related to sac programming (3)
		——*or*——	
	Six months	AA Degree or two years of college in related field or equivalent	Six credit hours: ■ child and youth development (3) ■ other areas related to sac programming (3)
		——*or*——	
	One year	AA Degree or two years of college in unrelated field	Six credit hours: ■ child and youth development (3) ■ other areas related to sac programming (3)
Group Leader	None	Bachelor's Degree in a related field	
		——*or*——	
	Three months	Bachelor's Degree in unrelated field	Three credit hours: ■ child and youth development
		——*or*——	
	Six months	AA Degree in related field	
		——*or*——	
	Nine Months	AA Degree or two years of college or equivalent	Three credit hours: ■ child and youth development
		——*or*——	
	Eighteen months	HS Diploma or GED	Six credit hours: ■ child and youth development (3) ■ other areas related to sac programming (3)
Assistant Group Leader	None	Minimum age: 16	See section on orientation and in-service training

DEFINITION OF QUALIFICATIONS TERMS

Experience	■ Related experience includes work with school-age children in a recreation, fine arts, camping, or academic setting. ■ One year's experience means full time (2,080 hours of work). The total number of hours can be from a combination of positions.
Professional preparation	■ This is formal post secondary training directly related to school-age childcare.
Administration courses	This includes courses such as: ■ Human resources management (e.g. supervision) ■ Fiscal management ■ Organizational development ■ Strategic planning ■ Marketing ■ Community development
Courses in SAC Programming	This includes courses such as: ■ Supervision ■ Health and safety ■ Developmentally appropriate practices ■ Guidance, including group and individual guidance ■ Community service and service learning ■ Working with families ■ Community outreach ■ Planning activities
Child and youth development	■ This includes courses that focus on development during middle childhood and early adolescence.
Related field	■ This includes majors in early childhood education, youth studies, child development, recreation, family social sciences, and elementary education.
Credit hours	■ These are credits for post-secondary coursework. ■ Each credit represents approximately 15 hours of participation in a course. ■ These may be earned through college classes, or as part of a post secondary technical/vocational certificate program.

APPENDIX TWO
STANDARDS AT A GLANCE

 Human Relationships

1. Staff relate to all children and youth in positive ways.

   a) Staff treat children with respect and listen to what they say.

   b) Staff make children feel welcome and comfortable.

   c) Staff respond to children with acceptance and appreciation.

   d) Staff are engaged with children.

2. Staff respond appropriately to the individual needs of children and youth.

   a) Staff know that each child has special interests and talents.

   b) Staff recognize the range of children's abilities.

   c) Staff can relate to a child's culture and home language.

   d) Staff respond to the range of children's feelings and temperaments.

3. Staff encourage children and youth to make choices and to become more responsible.

   a) Staff offer assistance in a way that supports a child's initiative.

   b) Staff assist children without taking control, and they encourage children to take leadership roles.

   c) Staff give children many chances to choose what they will do, how they will do it, and with whom.

   d) Staff help children make informed and responsible choices.

4. Staff interact with children and youth to help them learn.

    a) Staff ask questions that encourage children to think for themselves.

    b) Staff share skills and resources to help children gain information and solve problems.

    c) Staff vary the approaches they use to help children learn.

    d) Staff help children use language skills through frequent conversations.

5. Staff use positive techniques to guide the behavior of children and youth.

    a) Staff give attention to children when they cooperate, share, care for materials, or join in activities.

    b) Staff set appropriate limits for children.

    c) Staff use no harsh discipline methods.

    d) Staff encourage children to resolve their own conflicts. Staff step in only if needed to discuss the issues and work out a solution.

6. Children and youth generally interact with one another in positive ways.

    a) Children appear relaxed and involved with each other.

    b) Children show respect for each other.

    c) Children usually cooperate and work well together.

    d) When problems occur, children often try to discuss their differences and work out a solution.

7. Staff and families interact with each other in positive ways.

    a) Staff make families feel welcome and comfortable.

    b) Staff and families treat each other with respect.

    c) Staff share the languages and cultures of the families they serve, and the communities they live in.

    d) Staff and families work together to make arrivals and departures between home and childcare go smoothly.

8. Staff work well together to meet the needs of children and youth.

    a) Staff communicate with each other while the program is in session to ensure that the program flows smoothly.

    b) Staff are cooperative with each other.

    c) Staff are respectful of each other.

    d) Staff provide role models of positive adult relationships.

Indoor Environment

9. The program's indoor space meets the needs of children and youth.

   a) There is enough room for all program activities.

   b) The space is arranged well for a range of activities: physical games and sports, creative arts, dramatic play, quiet games, enrichment offerings, eating, and socializing.

   c) The space is arranged so that various activities can go on at the same time without much disruption.

   d) There is adequate and convenient storage space for equipment, materials, and personal possessions of children and staff.

10. The indoor space allows children and youth to take initiative and explore their interests.

    a) Children can get materials out and put them away by themselves with ease.

    b) Children can arrange materials and equipment to suit their activities.

    c) The indoor space reflects the work and interests of the children.

    d) Some areas have soft, comfortable furniture on which children can relax.

 Outdoor Environment

11. The outdoor play area meets the needs of children and youth, and the equipment allows them to be independent and creative.

    a) Each child has a chance to play outdoors for at least 30 minutes out of every three-hour block of time at the program.

    b) Children can use a variety of outdoor equipment and games for both active and quiet play.

    c) Permanent playground equipment is suitable for the sizes and abilities of all children.

    d) The outdoor space is suitable for a wide variety of activities.

Activities

12. The daily schedule is flexible, and it offers enough security, independence, and stimulation to meet the needs of all children and youth.

    a) The routine provides stability without being rigid.

    b) Children meet their physical needs in a relaxed way.

    c) Individual children move smoothly from one activity to another, usually at their own pace.

    d) When it is necessary for children to move as a group, the transition is smooth.

13. Children and youth can choose from a wide variety of activities.

    a) There are regular opportunities for active, physical play.

    b) There are regular opportunities for creative arts and dramatic play.

    c) There are regular opportunities for quiet activities and socializing.

    d) Children have a chance to join enrichment activities that promote basic skills and higher-level thinking.

14. Activities reflect the mission of the program and promote the development of all the children and youth in the program.

    a) Activities are in line with the styles, abilities, and interests of the individuals in the program.

    b) Activities are well suited to the age range of children in the program.

    c) Activities reflect the languages and cultures of the families served.

    d) Activities reflect and support the program's mission.

15. There are sufficient materials to support program activities.

    a) Materials are complete and in good repair.

    b) There are enough materials for the number of children in the program.

    c) Materials are developmentally appropriate for the age range of the children in the program.

    d) Materials promote the program's mission.

Safety, Health, & Nutrition

16. The safety and security of children and youth are protected.

    a) There are no observable safety hazards in the program space.

    b) Systems are in place to protect the children from harm, especially when they move from one place to another or use the rest room.

    c) Equipment for active play is safe.

    d) A system is in place to keep unauthorized people from taking children from the program.

17. The program provides an environment that protects and enhances the health of children and youth.

    a) The indoor and outdoor facilities are clean.

    b) There are no observable health hazards in the indoor or outdoor space.

    c) There are adequate supplies and facilities for handwashing.

    d) The heat, ventilation, noise level, and light in the indoor space are comfortable.

18. The program staff try to protect and enhance the health of children and youth.

    a) Staff are responsive to the individual health needs of the children.

    b) Staff protect children from communicable disease by separating children who become ill during the program.

    c) Staff protect children from potential hazards such as the following: caustic or toxic art materials and cleaning agents, medications, and hot liquids; overexposure to heat or cold.

    d) Staff and children wash hands frequently, especially after using the toilet or before preparing food.

19. Children and youth are carefully supervised to maintain safety.

    a) Staff note when children arrive, when they leave, and with whom they leave.

    b) Staff know where the children are and what they are doing.

    c) Staff supervise children appropriately according to children's ages, abilities, and needs.

    d) Staff closely supervise activities that are potentially harmful.

20. The program serves foods and drinks that meet the needs of children and youth.

    a) The program serves healthy foods.

    b) Drinking water is readily available at all times.

    c) The amount and type of food offered is appropriate for the ages and sizes of children.

    d) Snacks and meals are timed appropriately for children.

 ## Administration

21. Staff/child ratios and group sizes permit the staff to meet the needs of children and youth.

    a) Staff/child ratios vary according to the ages and abilities of children. The ratio is between 1:10 and 1:15 for groups of children age six and older. The ratio is between 1:8 and 1:12 for groups that include children under age six.

    b) Staff/child ratios and group sizes vary according to the type and complexity of the activity, but group sizes do not exceed 30.

    c) There is a plan to provide adequate staff coverage in case of emergencies.

    d) Substitute staff are used to maintain ratios when regular staff are absent.

22. Children and youth are supervised at all times.

    a) Children's arrivals are supervised.

    b) Children's departures are supervised.

    c) Staff have a system for knowing where the children are at all times.

    d) Staff plan for different levels of supervision according to the level of risk involved in an activity.

23. Staff support families' involvement in the program.

    a) There is a policy that allows family members to visit any time throughout the day.

    b) Staff offer orientation sessions for new families.

    c) Staff keep families informed about the program.

    d) Staff encourage families to give input and to get involved in program events.

24. Staff, families, and schools share important information to support the well-being of children and youth.

a) Program policies require that staff and family members communicate about the child's well-being.

b) Staff, families, and schools work together as a team to set goals for each child; they work with outside specialists when necessary.

c) Staff and families share information about how to support children's development.

d) Staff and families join together to communicate and work with the schools.

25. The program builds links to the community.

a) Staff provide information about community resources to meet the needs of children and their families.

b) The program develops a list of community resources. The staff draw from these resources to expand program offerings.

c) The staff plan activities to help children get to know the larger community.

d) The program offers community-service options, especially for older children.

26. The program's indoor space meets the needs of staff.

a) There is enough room in the indoor space for staff to plan various program activities.

b) Staff have access to adequate and convenient storage.

c) The indoor space meets or exceeds local health and safety codes.

d) Written guidelines are in place regarding the use and maintenance of the program facility.

27. The outdoor space is large enough to meet the needs of children, youth, and staff.

a) There is enough room in the outdoor space for all program activities.

b) The outdoor space meets or exceeds local health and safety codes.

c) Staff use outdoor areas to provide new outdoor play experiences.

d) There is a procedure in place for regularly checking the safety and maintenance of the outdoor play space.

28. Staff, children, and youth work together to plan and implement suitable activities, which are consistent with the program's philosophy.

   a) Staff ask children to share their ideas for planning so that activities will reflect children's interests.

   b) The program's daily activities are in line with its mission and philosophy.

   c) Staff keep on file their records of activity planning.

   d) Staff plan activities that will reflect the cultures of the families in the program and the broad diversity of human experience.

29. Program policies and procedures are in place to protect the safety of the children and youth.

   a) Staff and children know what to do in case of general emergency.

   b) The program has established procedures to prevent accidents and manage emergencies.

   c) The program has established policies to transport children safely; it complies with all legal requirements for vehicles and drivers.

   d) A system is in place to prevent unauthorized people from taking children from the program.

30. Program policies exist to protect and enhance the health of all children and youth.

   a) There is current documentation showing that the program has met the state and/or local health and safety guidelines and/or regulations.

   b) There are written policies and procedures to ensure the health and safety of children.

   c) No smoking is allowed in the program.

   d) The staff are always prepared to respond to accidents and emergencies.

31. All staff are professionally qualified to work with children and youth.

   a) Staff meet the requirements for experience with school-age children in recreational settings.

   b) Staff have received the recommended type and amount of preparation. They meet the requirements that are specific to school-age childcare and relevant to their particular jobs.

   c) Staff meet minimum age requirements.

   d) Enough qualified staff are in place to meet all levels of responsibility. Qualified staff are hired in all areas: to administer the program, to oversee its daily operations, and to supervise children.

32. Staff (paid, volunteer, and substitute) are given an orientation to the job before working with children and youth.

    a) A written job description that outlines responsibilities to children, families, and the program is reviewed with each staff member.

    b) Written personnel policies are reviewed with staff.

    c) Written program policies and procedures, including emergency procedures and confidentiality policies, are reviewed with staff.

    d) New staff are given a comprehensive orientation to the program philosophy, routines, and practices. They are personally introduced to the people with whom they will be working.

33. The training needs of the staff are assessed, and training is relevant to the responsibilities of each job. Assistant Group Leaders receive at least 15 hours of training annually. Group Leaders receive at least 18 hours of training annually. Senior Group Leaders receive at least 21 hours of training annually. Site Directors receive at least 24 hours of training annually. Program Administrators receive at least 30 hours of training annually.

    a) Staff receive training in how to work with families and how to relate to children in ways that promote their development.

    b) Program directors and administrators receive training in program management and staff supervision.

    c) Staff receive training in how to set up program space and design activities to support program goals.

    d) Staff receive training in how to promote the safety, health, and nutrition of children.

34. Staff receive appropriate support to make their work experience positive.

    a) The program has a plan in place to offer the best possible wages and working conditions in an effort to reduce staff turnover.

    b) Full-time staff receive benefits, including health insurance and paid leaves of absence. Staff are also given paid breaks and paid preparation time.

    c) Staff are given ample time to discuss their own concerns regarding the program.

    d) Staff receive continuous supervision and feedback. This includes written performance reviews on a timely basis.

35. The administration provides sound management of the program.

   a) The financial management of the program supports the program's goals.

   b) The administration oversees the recruitment and retention of program staff.

   c) The director involves staff, board, families, and children in both long-term planning and daily decision-making.

   d) Administrators assist with ongoing evaluation. They aim for improvement in all areas of the program.

36. Program policies and procedures are responsive to the needs of children, youth, and families in the community.

   a) A written mission statement sets forth the program's philosophy and goals.

   b) The program makes itself affordable to all families by using all possible community resources and sources of subsidy.

   c) The program's hours of operation are based on families' needs.

   d) It is the program's policy to enroll children with special needs.

Appendix Three

Glossary

Why did we include a glossary?

This glossary was written to clarify the meaning of certain terms and phrases used throughout the NAA Standards for Quality School-Age Care. We believe that the words and ideas below are important to the work we do as school-age professionals. We hope that these descriptions will help others to better understand the Standards so that they can be more successful in achieving them.

children and youth

The NAA Standards for Quality School-Age Care were developed for afterschool programs that serve children between the ages of five and fourteen. The words children and youth appear together in every Key. We hope this will reinforce the importance of creating a program that meets the needs of the oldest, as well as the youngest children in this age range. The term "children" appears alone in the Standards and Examples under each Key. This is done simply to avoid repetition. The word "children" refers to the older youth in our programs as well as the younger children.

community

Community refers to the city, town, or county where the program is located. Linking up with individuals and organizations in the community is a worthy goal for any program. People and groups in the area can help afterschool programs in many ways.

Community can also refer to a group of people who share a common culture, language, religion, or ethnic identity. Often, many smaller communities coexist within a city or town. Successful programs try to include the many communities around them. They value the special features of each culture and group. These programs try to reflect diversity in the demographic makeup of their staff. They also try to honor diversity in their policies, procedures, and activities.

culture

A program implements *culturally appropriate practices* when children are given a chance to learn about themselves and others by sharing cultural similarities and differences. Programs respond to cultural differences by encouraging staff to ask individuals and families from the community to help plan activities that represent various languages and cultural traditions. Staff try to learn more about different cultural styles. This helps them know how to respond to these differences in appropriate ways. A culturally responsive program seeks to involve and include families at all levels: in day-to-day discussion, in setting procedures, planning events, and in defining policy.

When staff understand children's home language and family backgrounds, children feel respected and valued. This approach is just as important in communities with little cultural diversity as it is in very diverse areas. Encouraging children to respect and appreciate differences helps them develop a more realistic view of society. It also teaches them to avoid prejudice and stereotypes.

developmentally appropriate practices

This phrase refers to program methods and goals that respond to the ages, developmental stages, and individual differences of children and youth. We all know that a child's interests and abilities change as she or he grows and matures. Research suggests that these changes usually occur within a series of predictable stages. The changes often affect a child's social, physical, emotional, and intellectual needs. It is important for school-age staff to understand the stages of development as well as the individual needs of children. Such knowledge will help staff relate to every person in the program. It will also help the staff plan activities that are well suited to children and youth at different stages of development.

family

There are a number of family types in today's school-age care programs. Staff will need to examine how they define the word "family." A new and broader definition of "family" may include: children and adults living in the home, adults who are responsible for the care and well-being of the child, parents who may not live in the same household as the child, and the child's legal guardian. Successful providers try to recognize and value the child's definition of family, even if it is different from the provider's experience.

full-time staff

In the field of school-age care, staff who work approximately 32 to 40 hours per week are generally considered full-time employees. Usually, full-time employees receive benefits such as: paid breaks, health insurance, paid sick days, and paid vacation days.

group size

This refers to children who are gathered together for a single purpose and are directly supervised by two or three staff. The group may gather for active games, team sports, group meetings, etc. More than one group may be engaged in an activity at the same time. For example, they may be playing on the playground, watching a performance, or riding a bus. In general, group size and makeup will keep changing because of new activity choices, or to meet the needs of individual children. We suggest that whenever possible, group sizes do not exceed thirty children.

indoor space, or environment

The indoor environment refers to the enclosed space where program activities take place. The indoor environment includes any room used by the program (e.g., cafeteria, library, gym, computer lab, classroom, recreation room, art studio). It may include nearby rooms or buildings where groups of children participate in activities (e.g., town library, dance studio, karate club, clay workshop). The environment also includes furniture, materials, and visual displays. We realize that many successful programs are located in very challenging spaces. We try to evaluate programs on how they use the space that is available to them. We recognize a program's efforts to use its space to its fullest potential. *(See also* program space.*)*

language differences

In many families, a language other than English is spoken in the home. It is important for afterschool programs to respond to a child's home language in appropriate ways. This can be accomplished through:

- staff members who speak the child's home language.
- peers who speak the child's home language.
- volunteers who can act as translators for family and staff (to avoid using children to translate for their parents whenever possible).
- providing written material and meetings in the home language of families.
- including materials such as books, music and books on tape in the child's home language.

Recognizing the home language of children will help them feel valued and respected. Research suggests that children who are able to fully develop their home language are better able to master English as a second language. Supporting the home language will actually help children learn English successfully. Please also refer to the section on promoting English language development under *mission*.

middle school youth

Studies have shown that children and youth who are unsupervised for long periods of time are more likely to find themselves in risky situations. Programs that can provide safe alternatives for older school-age children perform an important community service.

Youth between the ages of ten and fourteen want more challenge and independence than their younger peers. Successful programs offer these youth a range of activity choices: clubs, classes, field trips, workshops, etc. Often, youths will have their own space or "clubhouse" within the program. Older youth are given much more responsibility and "ownership" of their part of program. They need to be involved in planning, setting rules, and making decisions. However, they also need plenty of time just to "hang out" and socialize with their peers.

mission

A program's mission is based on its philosophy. A set of goals and an action plan support the program's mission. The activities and materials in a program make it possible to put the mission into practice. The examples in the chart below show how a program's activities are directly related to its mission. This list is meant as a starting point, and programs are encouraged to consider other possible missions not listed here. Because we feel that all missions have equal importance, we have chosen to list them in random order.

Mission	Activities

To support success in school;
To promote literacy; or
To promote English language
   development.
	The program helps children succeed with:
	■ hands-on activities that involve all of the senses
	  (touching, smelling, tasting, looking, and listening)
	■ props, gestures, and drawings to clarify meaning
	■ open-ended activities around a particular theme so
	  children can explore and learn at their own pace
	■ a buddy system to pair a child with strong skills with
	  a child whose abilities are developing
	
	Staff at the program help children by:
	■ praising their efforts, even when the pronunciation
	  or grammar isn't quite right
	■ setting the context for activities that rely heavily on
	  listening and speaking skills by surrounding them
	  with positive examples (conversation, songs, stories,
	  chants, plays, games, etc.)
	■ reducing the anxiety level by being accepting and
	  uncritical
	■ encouraging active participation in a non-
	  threatening environment
	
	The program encourages children to complete their
	homework. It provides:
	■ quiet study areas
	■ staff assistance
	■ cooperative learning
	■ peer tutoring
	■ remedial and practice sessions
	■ writing workshop (e.g., bookmaking, letter writing,
	  word processing)
	■ resources and materials for homework and projects
	  (e.g., books, magazines, library access)
	■ spelling/geography bees and games
	■ direct links to teachers and schools
	■ math manipulatives and challenges

To promote recreational, leisure activities.	**The program introduces children to a wide variety** **of hobbies:** ■ arts and crafts ■ cooking ■ music and dance ■ collecting ■ puzzles and games ■ travel ■ plants and animals

Mission	Activities
	The program includes a wide variety of sports activities: ■ team games ■ aerobic activities ■ exercise and fitness ■ skill practice ■ cooperative games
To support multicultural appreciation.	The program includes diverse cultures in offering: ■ books and storytelling ■ music and dance ■ snacks and cooking ■ sports and games ■ language and communication ■ speakers and guests ■ field trips ■ presentations ■ special events
To promote community involvement.	The program helps youth attend group meetings in the community: ■ 4H groups ■ Campfire Girls and Boys ■ Scouts ■ Junior Achievement The program sponsors Service Learning projects: ■ planting trees and gardens ■ recycling ■ volunteering at hospitals and nursing homes ■ organizing food/clothing drives ■ fund raising for worthy causes The program invites visitors to describe their work: ■ rescue-squad members ■ nurses ■ public health workers ■ veterinarians ■ firefighters ■ police officers The program visits local points of interest: ■ hospitals ■ libraries ■ businesses ■ senior centers ■ nursing homes ■ recycling facilities

Mission	Activities
	The program invites local citizens to describe their lives: ■ seniors ■ people with developmental or physical disabilities ■ experts on travel, cooking, gardening, etc. ■ community "heroes"—coaches, musicians, chefs, teachers, historians, artists, etc. The program helps children and youth engage in: ■ school projects ■ tutoring younger children ■ painting a school mural ■ playground cleanup ■ helping teachers with bulletin boards, etc.
To promote the arts (visual and performing).	The program arranges for: ■ field trips to museums and artists' studios ■ visits to dance and music rehearsals ■ attendance at local events ■ visiting artists ■ artists-in-residence The program helps children and youth: ■ write and present puppet shows, plays, talent shows, etc. ■ keep journals and records ■ share their talents with one another ■ perform for parents, younger children, nursing homes, etc.

Next Steps

This section of the *NAA Standards for Quality School-Age Child Care* contains a tool to help programs determine how to proceed. They may be ready to begin a full self-study, or they may choose to continue working on targeted improvements, using these Standards as a guide. The Next Steps section is located on page 67 of this book.

outdoor space, or environment

The outdoor environment refers to the open-air space where program activities take place. The outdoor environment includes program entrance and exit areas and all outdoor play spaces at the program site. It also may include nearby areas that children use, such as a local park, soccer field, outdoor swimming pool, tennis court, etc. We realize that some programs do not have a permanent outdoor play area. We hope that these programs will use outdoor areas within the program community.

philosophy

A program's philosophy states its principles and beliefs. The program bases its policies and practices on this philosophy. The statement is likely to explain how the program intends to promote the healthy development of children and youth. The statement sometimes describes the type of environment and experiences that the program hopes to create. A program needs to have a clear understanding of its philosophy before it can develop a mission statement.

program space

Space refers to the place where program activities occur. Some programs find space in a self-contained building (such as a church or a school). Other programs may use one large room (such as a gym or a cafeteria) that can be divided into activity areas. Program space may also include locations throughout the community where children engage in specialized activities, such as swimming, playing soccer, or taking music lessons. (*See also* indoor space, outdoor space.)

ratio

Ratios refer to the number of staff at the program compared to the number of children enrolled. Low ratios ensure that there are enough staff to maintain the safety and security of the children. Appropriate ratios also help create an environment where children feel emotionally secure. When there are enough adults to supervise a given group, the staff-to-child interactions can be more meaningful. Recommended licensing ratios vary from one state to the next. The numbers may be slightly higher or lower than the NAA ratios for accreditation. **The minimum ratios that must be met in order to achieve NAA Accreditation vary according to the ages and abilities of children. The ratio is between 1:10 and 1:15 for groups of children age six and older. The ratio is between 1:8 and 1:12 for groups that include children under age six.**

school-age care program

School-age program refers to an organization that provides care for children and youth between the ages of five and 14, during their out-of-school time. Successful afterschool programs work in cooperation with families to provide guidance, supervision, and support to the individuals in their care. The NAA Program Improvement and Accreditation (PIA) System seeks to include a broad range of program types. NAA hopes that this variety will make the hours before and after school more meaningful for children. Please refer to the sections on program philosophy and mission for examples of the types of programs that may choose to participate in the NAA PIA System.

special needs

It is important for school-age care programs to be inclusive and responsive to individual differences among children. Afterschool programs can meet the individual needs of each child by working closely with families, teachers, and specialists. This collaboration is crucial to make the program accessible to all children. Although each child is unique, programs may need to work with others to develop a plan to meet the special needs of an individual child. These needs might be physical, behavioral, medical, emotional, or cognitive; and may require that the child receive special assistance. The plan might include providing special materials, defining a behavior plan, training staff for medical needs, adapting the space to permit wheelchair access, etc. In order to become accredited, programs must show that they have a policy for enrolling children with special needs.

suspected child abuse, preventing and reporting

It is imperative that all school-age care staff understand their responsibility to report suspected cases of child abuse or neglect. School-age care programs should have written policies which clearly state the procedures for reporting such cases. Abusive treatment might include causing physical harm to a child; humiliating or degrading a child; inappropriate touching or verbal exchange with a child; mental cruelty; or withholding food, water, or basic care. To protect the safety and security of children and staff, programs should also have written policies aimed at preventing abuse from happening in the program, as well as policies to protect staff against unwarranted claims of abuse.

temperament

Temperament describes a person's disposition or nature. The intensity and range of a person's emotions are influenced by temperament. A person's temperament will define his or her activity level, regularity of bodily functions, and response to new situations or things. Temperament is also linked to a person's adaptability, quality of mood, attention span, and persistence. Individual differences in temperament are present from birth. They are thought to be hereditary, and they remain relatively consistent over time. However, individual experiences and development can affect temperament.

transitions

Transitions refer to those times when individuals or groups move from one place in the program to another. Transitions take place when individual children enter or exit the program and when a child has finished with an activity and chooses to move on to another. Children are in transition when they clean up or rearrange the space to prepare for a new activity. They are also in transition when they move from one area of the program (such as the cafeteria) to another area (such as the gym). It is important that transitions take place smoothly. Successful staff set clear expectations and provide adequate supervision at these times. In most successful programs, children move together as a group only when there is a clear reason for needing to do so.

NAA Publications Order Form

ITEM	QUANTITY	MEMBER	NON-MEMBER	TOTAL
NAA Standards for Quality School-Age Care	_____	$12 each	$15 each	$ _____
Shipping & Handling 1–3 ($5), 4–6 ($8), 7–10 ($12)	_____			$ _____
Standards at a Glance (brochure)	_____	$.45 each	$.50 each	$ _____
NAA Membership (complete form on following page)				$ _45__
Total Enclosed				$ _____

For bulk discount prices on orders over 10 books, please contact the NAA office 617.298.5012

SHIPPING ADDRESS:

Name _____

Street _____

City/State/Zip _____

METHOD OF PAYMENT:

❏ check enclosed ❏ purchase order # _____

Please charge my: ❏ VISA ❏ Mastercard

Card # _____ Exp. _____

Authorized Signature _____

BILLING ADDRESS:

Name _____

Street _____

City/State/Zip _____

MAIL TO:
NATIONAL AFTERSCHOOL ASSOCIATION
1137 WASHINGTON STREET, BOSTON, MA 02124
FAX 617-298-5022
PHONE 617-298-5012

Join this powerful national network of support for quality school-age care today!

You can become linked to the thousands of other people who are working to provide safe places for children and youth to learn and grow in their out-of-school time...*Join NAA today.*

MEMBER INVOLVEMENT:
Check the NAA activities in which you'd like to take part:

❏ public policy
❏ professional development
❏ leadership development
❏ program accreditation

❏ conference
❏ Board recruitment
❏ communications
❏ member services

❏ Do not publish my name in an NAA directory for members only.

From time to time, NAA makes its mailing list available to groups whose services or products are of potential benefit to our members.
❏ Check here if you do not want your name shared in this way.

NAME _____ ❏ NEW MEMBER ❏ RENEWAL

ORGANIZATION _____

JOB TITLE _____

STREET _____

CITY / STATE / ZIP_____

PHONE _____

E-MAIL _____

REFERRED BY _____

**MAIL THIS APPLICATION WITH THE
$45 ANNUAL MEMBERSHIP FEE PAYABLE TO "NAA" TO:**
NATIONAL AFTERSCHOOL ASSOCIATION
1137 WASHINGTON STREET, BOSTON, MA 02124
FAX 617-298-5022
PHONE 617-298-5012

NAA Publications Order Form

ITEM	QUANTITY	MEMBER	NON-MEMBER	TOTAL
NAA Standards for Quality School-Age Care	_____	$12 each	$15 each	$ _____
Shipping & Handling 1–3 ($5), 4–6 ($8), 7–10 ($12)	_____			$ _____
Standards at a Glance (brochure)	_____	$.45 each	$.50 each	$ _____
NAA Membership (complete form on following page)				$ 45
Total Enclosed				$ _____

*For bulk discount prices on orders over 10 books,
please contact the NAA office 617.298.5012*

SHIPPING ADDRESS:

Name _____

Street _____

City/State/Zip _____

METHOD OF PAYMENT:

❏ check enclosed   ❏ purchase order # _____

Please charge my: ❏ VISA   ❏ Mastercard

Card # _____ Exp. _____

Authorized Signature _____

BILLING ADDRESS:

Name _____

Street _____

City/State/Zip _____

MAIL TO:
NATIONAL AFTERSCHOOL ASSOCIATION
1137 WASHINGTON STREET, BOSTON, MA 02124
FAX 617-298-5022
PHONE 617-298-5012

Join this powerful national network of support for quality school-age care today!

You can become linked to the thousands of other people who are working to provide safe places for children and youth to learn and grow in their out-of-school time...*Join NAA today.*

MEMBER INVOLVEMENT:
Check the NAA activities in which you'd like to take part:

❏ public policy
❏ professional development
❏ leadership development
❏ program accreditation

❏ conference
❏ Board recruitment
❏ communications
❏ member services

❏ Do not publish my name in an NAA directory for members only.

From time to time, NAA makes its mailing list available to groups whose services or products are of potential benefit to our members.
❏ Check here if you do not want your name shared in this way.

NAME _____ ❏ NEW MEMBER ❏ RENEWAL

ORGANIZATION _____

JOB TITLE _____

STREET _____

CITY/STATE/ZIP_____

PHONE _____

E-MAIL _____

REFERRED BY _____

MAIL THIS APPLICATION WITH THE $45 ANNUAL MEMBERSHIP FEE PAYABLE TO "NAA" TO:

NATIONAL AFTERSCHOOL ASSOCIATION
1137 WASHINGTON STREET, BOSTON, MA 02124
FAX 617-298-5022
PHONE 617-298-5012